Patty Jacobs

My Balancing Act

© 2010 by Patty Jacobs
All rights reserved.

ISBN 978-0-9763016-1-5

This book may be ordered at Lulu.com, Amazon.com, Barnesandnoble.com and book retail stores.

Design by Niki Harris Graphic Design
Eugene, Oregon

Cover illustration by James Cloutier

for Wes

"Not knowing when dawn will come I open every door." Emily Dickinson

Acknowledgments

First I want to acknowledge the great support, help, and patience my family have given me over three decades of learning to live a promising future with MS. My deep appreciation for guidance, reading, clarification, editing, and sustenance go to many: Cecelia Hagen, a fine teacher, mentor, and editor; Niki Harris, whose invaluable editing, organization and completed design helped my stories hang together; James Cloutier, for a happy likeness on the cover; and my neurologist, Dr. Ray Englander, whose knowledge and watchful eye has always been a great help in keeping the progression of my disease at bay.

Contents

13	Foreword
21	Facing the Facts
31	An Unforgettable Summer
41	Determination and Optimism
49	The Youngest Son
57	An Awakening
65	Water, My Balancing Act
75	Esprit
85	Waiting and Thinking
99	Fur and Choices
105	Artful Encounters
115	My Dream House
123	Kayaking, Friendship, and Fate
131	Down Ford Way
139	Kipu Ranch Adventure
149	Wake Up Call

Foreword

Some 30 years ago I faced the most difficult period in my life, when our son David's diagnosis of schizophrenia at age 20 coincided with my onset of MS. Together and yet alone, David and I were torn apart by the uncertainty of our futures and the courses our diseases would take. My husband Wes and I felt gripped by compelling circumstances that needed our constant care and attention: Over the next four years, both of Wes's parents would pass away, my brother Larry would die of chronic leukemia, and my own parents would be in a near-fatal car accident that resulted in grave and strung-out health issues for both of them. My life was re-defined by adversity beyond my control. At times I wondered whether I would make it. As fate would have it, I found writing and water exercise my two saving graces. I felt drawn to the calmness that being in or near water had afforded me in the past, and I began putting pen to paper. Those two activities became the emotional and physical outlets that helped me in keep my sanity and changed the course of my tumultuous life for the good.

During the ten years that David was hospitalized I kept a journal in which I wrote mostly about him. Putting my feelings and fears down on paper relieved some anxiety about my own tenuous health and about how our family was being affected by the continuing turmoil. Some years ago I threw away those journals and started writing in earnest, approaching my computer or piece of paper as more than simply a way to relieve tension. I went to writing workshops at Cannon Beach, Menucha on the Columbia River Gorge, and later in Santa Fe, New Mexico.

When I reflect on the years I've spent writing, what comes to mind are the amazing and talented people I've met. Many have become confidants and close friends—people that I wouldn't otherwise have known. Along with Wes and my extended family, these fellow writers, teachers, and friends have guided and encouraged me to develop my skills, grow as a person, and overcome the obstacles of my disease.

At Haystack, a Cannon Beach workshop, I met Beverly Partridge—then a recently retired teacher, journalist, painter, and poet. Although her achievements are way beyond me, she remains a model of discipline, direction, and pacing. With fatigue as an overriding factor in people with MS (me for sure), pacing comes right after eating and sleeping. Beverly's example of how to prioritize is something that helps me almost every day.

Over 20 years ago I took a University of Oregon writing class from Cecelia Hagen. Cecelia is one of the most inspirational and encouraging teachers I've had in my adult life. Her calm demeanor, personal talent, and poetic background have helped to reinforce what Wes calls my can-do mind-set and to improve my confidence enough to publish my first book-length memoir, "Letters From England," in 2006. The idea of composing a novel remains tucked under the bed while I continue with two writing groups born out of Haystack and Cecelia's classes.

Kwinnim, my first writing group, has been meeting for several decades. Besides Beverly, the members (some now gone) are: Hannah Wilson, a teacher with the patience of Job; Quinton Hallett, with her Vassar education and worldly knowledge; Katherine Chase, with whom I shared my disease and our hopes for courage; Evelyn Hess, who is proving to me that life can be natural, green, and as full as its maker; and Barbara Engel, a woman who lives daily with a free spirit and giving nature. At a recent retreat, Barbara and I covered the Siltcoos Lagoon Trail on the Central Oregon Coast—I on my battery-powered wheelchair, Barbara at my side. We watched two nutria playing water tag, a noisy kingfisher, and the Great Blue Heron resting on a snag in the quiet lagoon. With friends like Barbara, anything is possible!

My life list of amazing friends and fellow writers continues, including poet Miriam Starlin, and the members of Cecelia's "Meadowlarks" memoir group—which has been meeting for over six years. The group is comprised of Laurel, Giny, Barbara, Sally, Heidi, Jo, and last but not least, Fred. Thanks to these outstanding compatriots, I'm working on layering my current writing with more introspection. I've become less judgmental and more sympathetic in my feelings towards some family members. Although my brother, Larry, died 25 years ago and was married and gone from my life the same length of time before that, I'm realizing what an important role he played in my early life: his spirited teasing was a major plus that encouraged my sense of humor. More importantly, Larry's love of the outdoors and willingness to have his little sister tag along made a snow skier, hiker, and water-sport enthusiast of me.

 Writing has become my back-home companion, and, as fellow Meadowlark and friend Sally says, "Writing about people who are no longer here brings them to life again." Family and friends I've loved and miss are with me still. I've been able to share and relive many great past adventures. Most significantly, writing has been a source of comfort when I'm worried or in a quandary. Writing doesn't substitute for a friend's soft shoulder, but, like a good book, it's always at one's elbow when needed.

 This collection of essays and memories is an attempt to delve into a period of my life where good fortune and exceptional opportunities vied with outbursts of feelings and difficult circumstances for both me and my family. I hope the reader will move back and forth along the spectrum of possibilities I've offered, gaining insight into a life that has been peppered with challenges and unforeseeable rewards.

Move and the way will open. —Zen saying

1

Facing the Facts

I woke up with a start one night soon after receiving my diagnosis of MS. I had dreamed I was a girl again, standing with Mother in the kitchen of the house I grew up in. *'No matter what happens to you in your life, you'll be able to handle it,'* she said. Every single day I give her thanks for her unconditional love and faith in me. During the last six months that we lived in England and in the early years following my diagnosis, I needed every speck of the courage for which she gave me credit.

My mother was religiously principled, even self-sacrificing. She had a genuine concern for others, including family and friends with physical needs. She cared for her arthritic mother with painstaking devotion for a dozen years after Grandpa died. She spent hours with her childless, widowed friend Dot, and felt in some way accountable when Dot committed suicide. Naive as I was back then, I never considered that my MS diagnosis may have been as devastating to Mother as it was to me. She kept that fact hidden from me.

Mother's strengths were catching. Among the tangibles that she passed on were a love of nature and the outdoors. The memories I have of camping trips when we hiked, picked huckleberries, dug clams, and even ran from a black bear on a switchback above Spirit Lake, Washington, still make me smile. During WWII half our back yard, about 30 by 15 feet, was planted in a "victory garden." I probably did more picking than tending, but the thrill of watching a sunflower I'd sewn grow way above me instilled a life-long love of gardening. Picking beans, raspberries, and canning salmon alongside my mother was anything but routine. She had a way of turning methodical chores into satisfying recreation. The in-house smell of forced daphne in February, the crocus and daffodil shoots showing through a sprinkle of snow, and the witch hazel budding rust-orange in my back yard—all of these marvels she taught me to look for during winter days.

David and Tom were both at school one sunny morning when my friend Ruth and I met at the Mildenhall Base tennis court to play singles. I served first and we began to volley. When I tried to run to the net for a short ball, my legs simply wouldn't move. I wasn't tired, winded, or hurting. I remember a weird weak feeling, and a tingling sensation that began at the top of my head and flashed down my spine like a tiny charge of electricity.

"Are you okay?" Ruth asked.

"Something's wrong. My legs won't go," I said, taking stiff, baby steps toward the net. The numbness was a first. Inside my head a dozen cat's eyes seemed to be glowing.

I tried to bend my legs and knees, to shake them. Something was wrong with my left leg. I took several deep breaths and tried to pull myself together. The flashing, numbing sensation muted temporarily. I walked slowly off the court.

"Let me drive you home. Someone can pick up your car later," Ruth said, sounding as scared as I felt.

With false bravado I said, "I'll be okay. I'll take it easy going home and call you when I get there."

By the time Wes and the boys came home for dinner I was better, although it seemed as if my whole body had slipped into low gear. When I told Wes what happened he asked how I'd slept the previous night, joking about my having had a second glass of wine. That night we went for an after-dinner walk through the village toward Devil's Dike, built during Roman times. I started up an incline with Wes behind me. I caught my left foot on a tree root in the trail and almost fell. A few steps later I tripped again and grabbed his arm. I had to consciously lift my left leg and swing it a bit to move forward.

"Stop a minute! Your foot's dropping. I think we better backtrack and take the shortest way home," he said. "Don't hurry, honey. I want to call Ray tonight when we get home and have him see you first thing in the morning."

Major Ray Englander was a young neurologist from New York with a citified background (his parents were both classical musicians). Ray had freckles, rusty-wavy hair, and a cute Mickey Rooney smile that hadn't gone unnoticed by the single women on the base.

"What's going on with you?" he said calmly. I told him about my tennis fiasco and mentioned that after a hot shower I had trouble walking down the long hall to our bedroom without hanging onto the wall.

"What else?" Ray asked.

"Well, there've been a few pretty disconcerting things happening to me over the past few months." He frowned slightly and nodded, waiting for me to continue. "Without feeling winded, I'm having trouble walking up hills," I said. "Plus, I took an embarrassing nosedive through the front door of a beer garden in Heidelberg last month. We were visiting Doug at school. I'm sure the other customers thought I'd had one too many."

"It sounds worrisome," he said.

"If I get down on my haunches to reach into a low kitchen cupboard, I can't get back up. I am exhausted by a hot shower in the morning and can barely make it down the long hallway. But the worst is my bladder—one cup of coffee in the morning goes through me in less than an hour. I can tell you the location of every loo in East Anglia!"

"I'm going to do a few preliminary tests. Then we'll schedule you in this week. We'll need several days."

I'm thankful Ray was the first doctor I saw in 1978.

He guided me through every neurological test available on the Lakenheath Base in a patient, kind, and methodical manner.

I had wires attached to my head while I stared at a flashing black and white checkerboard screen. Ray must have looked in my eyes a million times with his ophthalmoscope—clicking lenses and flashing lights till I felt like my entire head was translucent. He hammered on my knees, ankles, and wrists. I followed his pointing finger with my eyes, back and forth, up and down. He watched me walk toe-to-heel, heel-to-toe and try to hop—neither worked— and try to squat with no luck.

"This is awful," I said to Ray, wanting to run somewhere and hide and bawl my eyes out. I was sick of everyone (technicians, nurses, friends) telling me how brave I was being when, in fact, I felt like a kid again, hating the shots and tests. *It hurts! I'll never walk again. What if I fall and my legs are too weak to pick me up?*

After several days of appointments, Ray said, "Before we talk about your test results, I'd like to have Wes with us." Wes was waiting outside the door. We sat across the desk from him.

"You've been through every examination available here. I've scheduled you to see Dr. Yealland at Addenbrooks Hospital in Cambridge. He's head of the department of neurology. He'll have a new procedure done on you, a CAT scan. The scanner takes pictures of your spine and brain. Some of the same tests I've done will be repeated. Since Addenbrooks is a teaching hospital, there'll be student participation. It'll take several days and repeated tests. Are you okay with that?"

"Yes," I said softly, trying to swallow the tears that lay waiting every time I opened my mouth.

Student participation meant question after question.

"Did you have pets in your childhood home?"

"Yes. We had cocker spaniels. I remember kissing my dog, Rusty, and he'd lick me back."

"Did you have a childhood illness that confined you to bed?"

"Yes. When I was in third grade I had strep throat. I was in bed for six weeks. The doctor came to our house every week to shoot penicillin in my hip."

"Have you always lived in a Northern climate?"

"Yes, except for 18 months in California when I was twenty-eight."

"Can you pinpoint the onset other than when you were playing tennis?"

"Several times before that, when I was very tired or emotionally upset, I'd feel a zinging flash, like an electric shock that started at the top of my head and went all the way down my spine."

"What kinds of things upset you?"

"I'd rather not say."

After the tests were completed at Addenbrooks, Wes and I were summoned to Ray's office again.

"The tests you've been given the past few days lead to

one of two possibilities. Your symptoms point to multiple sclerosis: foot drop, tingling and numbness, incontinence, sensitivity to heat, fatigue," Ray said. "Nothing shows in your upper body. Your eyes are fine. Good sign, since partial blindness is often the case with MS. The other possibility is a spinal tumor."

"Which do you think it is?" I asked as Wes handed me his hanky and took hold of my hand.

"I wish I knew, Patty. You're fortunate to be in the right place at the right time. The CAT scan will give us the answers we need. Then we'll decide how to proceed," Ray said.

I lay on the living-room sofa watching the window for Tom's school bus. Self-pity hovered over me like the cream-soup fog outside on that late November afternoon. My friend Emily had stopped in with a potted yellow freesia that smelled like spring and made me wonder about my new wait-and-see-how-it-progresses disease. The scan had ruled out a spinal tumor. *At least I'm not going to die of cancer.*

Ray explained the two common forms of MS: exacerbating and remitting, which usually occurred between the ages of 20 and 40; and chronic progressive (now called primary progressive), which is a slower and less severe, more typical in people over forty (I was forty-one).

For the next five months I teeter-tottered between denial and anger, trying to pretend all was well, at least in public. The facts were that a slow quarter mile on flat ground was about as far as I could walk, and I was tired all the time. Wes, being realistic, cancelled our plan to take one last ski trip to the French Alps before we returned to the States.

"Don't worry about disappointing the boys," he said, brushing his lips over the back of my hand. "We can ski all we want in Oregon." *You can. The boys will. I mightn't be able even to cross-country.* I thought about climbing to the top of Mt. St. Helens with my brother, Larry, and writing 'Hi, Mom' in the crusty August snow. I thought about my summer as hike master at the Longview YMCA Camp, Spirit Lake, when I was twenty. I thought about backpacking with Wes and our sons in Oregon's Three Sisters Wilderness and swimming in icy glacial lakes.

Part of the Kubler-Ross's denial stage, "This can't be happening to me," lasted longer than I'd like to admit. But if someone so much as snapped their fingers, I would burst into tears.

My anger kicked in big time when we returned to Eugene. I jealously watched trails crowded with joggers along the Willamette River. I was unable to tolerate folks who made decisions for my welfare without consulting me, and I hated my ever-present feelings of exclusion and envy. As my grief subsided over my inability to participate in most of the outdoor activities I'd enjoyed, I rallied and began moving closer to a new way of living.

"No matter what happens…" Thank you, Mom. With Wes at my side and you in my heart, life is good.

2

An Unforgettable Summer

When we were preparing to return to Eugene after our three years in England, I wrote the following letter to my parents:

> *I've mailed a tape that I hope will arrive soon after this letter giving details from the CAT scan and tests I had in Cambridge. The news isn't as bad as it might have been. My neurologist says forty-one is old for Chronic Progressive Multiple Sclerosis. If the diagnosis is correct, I shouldn't be too disabled.*
>
> *I guess what I want to ask of you and other family and friends is to treat me like you always have. I plan to carry on with my life and do as much as I can after seeing what my limitations are. I hope you'll feel comfortable*

telling others about my disease—after all it can't be helped.

You know how I love to read and my eyes are just fine! I'm still the very same person I've always been—a very very fortunate daughter, wife, and mother…

In spite of my fervent wish to be treated normally, the biggest hitch for my parents, friends, and myself came on like a swirling wind, leaving no doubt that I was a different being. Unlike the passing of a tornado, the damage to my central nervous system and, thus, my self-image was permanent. I longed for some privacy and a comfortable place to lounge while struggling with the realities and restrictions of my illness (foot drop, fatigue, lack of balance, and overall weakness).

Coming home was one of the most difficult periods of my life. For starters our family was temporarily housed in a tenured University rental where we were baby sitting a neurotic Norwegian elk hound named Knut. Knut had a barking snit whenever Wes got closer to me than two feet. Almost as unforgiving was the house's hard-wearing Danish furniture, upholstered in an itchy burlap fabric. I'm sure it was chosen to prevent snuggling and/or scoliosis in anyone over six feet tall.

Why I agreed to let Lisa, our goddaughter, live with us that summer, with all three sons at home, is beyond me. Probably my goody-two-shoes attitude hadn't yet learned to make allowances for a weaker me. My annoyance festered when Lisa spent the entire two months she was there while attending the University of Oregon's summer school locked in her bedroom, studying, or chalking up long-distance calls to her Boston boyfriend. Every time she picked at a meal and one of the boys made a comment like, 'Lisa doesn't like green peppers', I chided myself for being duped on the one hand and feeling sorry for her on the other, since her father's financial support hinged on her summer school performance.

Remembering that difficult period of transitions and trauma, I always find a bright spot when I recall thirteen-year-old Tom's patience and unexpected solicitude. He had been with me daily from the onset of my MS and was more insightful and helpful than his age would indicate. He was the only kid in the house who acknowledged my physical weakness and my all-consuming need for rest.
"Take the phone off the hook and take a nap, Mom," Tom would say, noting my drawn expression. "I'll take Knut for a walk."
But sleep was elusive. I would lie awake exhausted, worrying about everything I couldn't control. Our eldest son, Doug, was up at 4:00 a.m. to leave for his job setting choker for a gypo logging company. Nineteen-year-old David was coming in after midnight from his restaurant job at the Quarterdeck with an aggressive girlfriend in hot pursuit. Tom was apprehensive about starting junior high and making new friends. Wes' mother was dealing with newly diagnosed ALS, and Knut barked day and night at the constantly ringing phone. I blamed MS for the tears

I experienced frequently and without warning. It was no wonder the older, preoccupied kids kept their distance except at mealtimes.

I was worn out by caring for four teenagers and worried about my floundering strength. My ambivalence toward my responsibilities was new and scary. Along with those worries was an all-consuming "why-me, there-must-be-a-reason" syndrome. I was all too ready to accept the logical fallacy of illness causing doom — *post hoc ergo propter hoc. Has the wholeness of the first half of my life ended forever?*

Wes was dealing with the stress of his new job. Outwardly, he covered up much of his concern for his mother's and my illnesses. Or maybe my new self-centeredness didn't allow me to see the angst that he had to be feeling. Besides being the captain with a steadfast hand who kept a semblance of normalcy during those months, he was the promoter and provider of my early mobility aids—I'll call them milestones, both needed and resented: a jade-handled walking stick that I tried to pretend wasn't necessary, an automatic transmission car with a handbrake, and later my Amigo electric wheelchair. Wes knew that my ability to drive gave me a chance, however temporary, to escape the chaos both at home and in my head.

When driving our manual station wagon before leaving England, it became evident to me that an automatic transmission was necessary: my weak left leg had a frightening tendency to slip off the clutch. I was lucky to limp out of the country accident free. So on our return to Eugene and without ruffling too many of my diffident feathers, my husband made an appointment with a company that does van conversions in Brownsville, Oregon.

Armed with the proper gear—a hand brake and a lift for my scooter in a new Chrysler mini-van, I got a sales job at Valentine Travel that helped me continue to make return trips to England and Scotland and to near and far destinations with my family.

Wes recalls my first meeting with Lyle, the Amigo distributor from Portland, as defiant.

"You were out to prove that no wheelchair could possibly work for you. You rode that scooter onto the street, turned it around, and headed for the curb full tilt, flipping it over before Lyle's startled eyes." In later years, after several more scooters and minor crashes over tree roots and inclines, Wes suggested to Lyle that the Amigo Company might like to hire me as a test driver.

Hard as family and friends tried and with varying degrees of aplomb, the cane and electric wheelchair left no room for denying my problem. Life continued to be touch and go, and like it or not, folks treated me differently. Wes' support, my extended family, and a constructive shrink helped move me forward to begin a new approach to living. Back then a psychiatrist pointed out that I was grieving for all the things I could no longer do, and she was right.

Several years after our return, my friend Katherine was also diagnosed with chronic progressive MS. A mutual acquaintance had introduced us with the notion that I was doing well and might be able to help her. The progression of MS is different in everyone. My weakness stayed in my lower extremities and affected my balance. Hers was more rapid and debilitating. Our close friendship helped us both and continued over several decades, leading to many discussions of the whys and wherefores of living with MS.

Katherine was a woman who spent her life putting everyone's needs ahead of her own. When her son Tim died in a scuba-diving accident, her physician gave her a limited prescription for sleeping pills. She halved the medication, shared it with her husband and other family members, and ran out before she personally benefited.

Whenever I ignored physical demands or gave in to self-imposed "shoulds," Wes would remind me, "The best thing you can do for the boys and me is to take care of yourself."

So when Katherine asked what the biggest difference was between us, I chose my words carefully and wasn't completely honest.

"You're more cautious than I am," I said.

Both of us had tenacious personalities, but that's where our likeness ended. I couldn't any more change what Wes called my cavalier approach to caution in dealing with MS and life than she could purposely tip a kayak over in a cold lake.

The end of that unforgettable summer is blurred in my mind, smeared with the grievances that have long since slipped into the fog of resentments surrounding the uncontrollable circumstances of those months. Wes' mother died the weekend we were to move from the rental to our new home. Of course he left immediately for Portland to be with his father and sister.

How my sons and I managed to transfer our household goods from the rental to our new place, I still wonder. We had no help from Lisa, whose boyfriend from Boston showed up two weeks before the move. She fled when I wouldn't let him become another live-in mouth to feed.

Somehow I muddled through. After time the same effective traits that I've attributed to my red-headed brother—optimism, determination, and resiliency began to take hold in me again, and I could look to the future with hope. My need for independence guided me forward, limpingly at first. I began to feel less like an invalid and couldn't abide being treated like one. Thus I had difficulty with people, however well-meaning, who felt they needed to take care of me. My friendships couldn't help but be affected.

But always in the back of my mind were my Mother's words reminding me: *No matter what happens, I will be able to handle it.* I was determined to move beyond the grief that I felt at losing much of my physical ability and to search for new and rewarding experiences. I took a writing class at the university from Cecelia Hagen, a great teacher and mentor.

Surrounded by stimulating associations with writers who became life-long friends, I began to try my hand with paper and pen.

That worked so well that now, tempered by a more modest, closer-to-home travel itinerary, an ongoing women's book club, and a study group, I'm ever ready to pack a notebook into what Mother called a grip and be off on another restorative journey.

3

Determination and Optimism

The Random House dictionary defines "optimism" as "a disposition or tendency to look on the more favorable side of conditions and to expect the most favorable outcome." "Determination" is "the quality of being resolute; firmness of purpose."

Optimism and determination are among the most lasting and defining things I inherited from my parents—my if-there's-a-will-there's-a-way attitude. During the toughest times in my life, I've tried to maintain an overall sense of well-being. My dad had what I would call a "head in the sand" sense that good always overcomes evil. He felt that you make your own good luck, and his was always around the next corner. The reader may sense some of this attitude in me!

Mother's life was set when she agreed to Dad's marriage proposal with the vaguest response imaginable.

She reportedly said, "I think so maybe," but she finally gave in, bucking her parents objections—no small feat considering her unassertive personality. She dedicated the rest of her life to being the best wife, homemaker, and mother possible, following the mores of her time persistently and unselfishly at her own expense.

So I became the sheltered second child of Depression-era folks who were forced to fall back on my mother's parents in 1932, when Dad lost his job with Shell Oil Company and Mother was pregnant with my brother, Larry. My parents had moved to Portland, Oregon after their marriage on April 18, 1929, following a lavish home wedding and reception in Longview, Washington, and dancing afterward in the third-floor ballroom of her parent's house. Their "silver-spoon" and presumably blissful early years came to a screeching halt when the Great Depression hit.

The stories Dad loved to tell and retell about that time had a less than subtle message.

"I started off on the wrong foot with your mother and learned the hard way that fibbing doesn't work," he said. "Like the dog-eared corner of a book, the story keeps opening to the same page, even after you're on to a new chapter."

Dad described the dark, wet autumn when he was laid off and didn't tell Mom—waiting in employment lines and sloshing the streets all day with nothing but rejections.

"There were thousands of guys like me, wandering around with their lunch pails hidden under their coats. Sometimes I hung out at the lot next to Westminster

Presbyterian, sitting on a bench, thinking about tucking inside to get warm since some of my hard-earned money paid for heating the damn place," he said, blowing his nose like a foghorn into his hanky.

"When an elder and a deacon from church called on your mother one afternoon, knowing I wouldn't be home, I hit the wall. They had the gall to tell her our pledge was three months in arrears and asked her for a check for the amount due. When I came home she was bawling her eyes out. I tried to hug her but she turned her back on me."

"'I'm sick of being kept in the dark! Why did you tell me you'd paid all the bills?'" your mother said. "I swore then and there I'd never set foot in that damn church again!"

"It might have been the next morning that your mother asked me to pick up a tin of tuna, eggs, and a quart of milk on my way home from work. All I had in my pocket was the $5 gold piece my dad gave me for graduation. What was left of it—and my luck—was in the bottom of the grocery sack. I came home determined to fess up and told your mother point blank, 'I'm flat broke and out of work.'"

So my parents left Portland and returned to Longview. Mother became the reluctant bookkeeper and go-between with her father, who loaned them money to buy a Mobil Station on the corner of 12th and Hudson. Dad swallowed his pride and spent the rest of life determined to get it back.

It seems I was a determined four-year-old swimmer, following my father into an icy mountain lake or a local river with the aplomb of an older kid. Dad was a tall, former competitive swimmer—fun to watch and attempt to copy.

I remember him teaching me strokes at the swimming hole at Lysons Park on the Coweeman River. He showed me the crawl and how to breathe, the breast and side stroke, and my favorite, the back stroke.

Recently on Kauai I snorkeled next to a seven-year-old with the same kind of determination I'd like to think I had at that age. The sun was just coming up as the Sea Rider's bootstrap-skinned Capt. Tara, introduced all of us who'd signed up for the three-hour, snorkel/whale-watching trip.

"We have two special people with us today," she said in a brassy twang. "Cloe, our seven-year-old-first-timer from Chicago, and Patty, an old hat with MS."

"Okay to tell about MS?" she asked, with an affirmative 'okay by you?' nod.

"Sure!" I said. "I'll need all the help I can get climbing back into the boat with my gear on."

When I had called to reserve a space on what was billed as a former US Navy SEAL rubber boat excursion, I said I had MS, but didn't mention my age. I've' learned that admitting to one drawback is enough said.

"I've snorkeled before. My problem will be getting out of the ocean and back in the boat," I said.

"There's a ladder and a strong hand on board. You'll be fine," the receptionist said. "We provide lunch and all the gear you'll need."

The first snorkel was in water at least 20 feet deep and lasted over a half hour. There were amazing schools of butterflyfish—golden, blue-striped, and brilliant orange—

feeding and foraging in an out of the coral. We saw thousands of parrotfish, brilliant yellow tangs, and two sea turtles on that first swim, one close enough to touch. Not a whine out of Cloe when Tara tightened the strap to the mask and pulled it over her long hair or a whimper when her missing front teeth hampered the seal on her snorkel. Had I been lying on that float with my face in the ocean at her age —Dad and Tara to guide me—I'm sure I would have been every bit as thrilled.

"Did you see a turtle?" I asked Cloe after that first swim. She was wrapped in a beach towel, shivering in her father's arms.

"No, but I saw a yellow fish and a black-and-white striped one," she said with a smile and a chattering lisp.

The boat ride was a white-knuckle affair over huge ocean swells. Cloe's dad was too seasick to go in a second time to look for sea turtles, but that little kid was back in the water on her board with Capt. Tara, showing the same traits of stubborn endurance attributed to all Taureans like me. I wondered if Cloe and I share the same star sign?

I confess that I met my match in that galloping contraption. Should I have a chance to snorkel again, I'll go for a big motor-going sailboat or yacht with a large stepladder and plenty of strong arms to pull me aboard. Then again, how would I have known what a poor choice I'd made if I hadn't given it a try.

By the time I was in high school my father made it clear that I should prepare for a career in one of the following fields: nursing, secretarial science, or teaching. I chose the latter in spite of my high school literature teacher, Mrs. Ann Donnelly, a busybody with permanently creased brows who peered over the top of her glasses, looking disdainfully down at me when she asked a question like, "Who wrote *The Scarlet Letter*?"

When I answered, "Nathaniel Hawthorne," she'd nod and frown, and I felt disapproved, even though I'd given the right answer. I've never forgotten the crack she made to Mom:

"Patty will never graduate from college. She's too boy crazy."

I wasn't aware of a *Mr.* Donnelly, and I gave myself license to call her a bitch (under my nice-girl breath). She had two sons, substituted in my mother's bridge group, and almost ruined my favorite subject. Her comment stayed with me through the rest of my dating life and on to a BS from Oregon State, a teaching job with the Portland Public Schools, and a 52-year marriage.

In addition to the traits I inherited, there were certain unquestionable givens in my family, expectations that were never spoken. These assumptions included: college follows high school; nice girls don't get pregnant; if the unthinkable happened, a girl would be stuck in a tedious life and with the wrong husband. Pregnancy meant marriage and marriage meant forever.

That line of thinking colored my relationship with my boyfriends. If a date became more than just that and didn't take no for an answer or suggested going steady, my avoidance instinct kicked in. This mind set became a near-reality during a ticklish situation my sophomore year at OSU. I wasn't about to accept when John, an AG major from La Grande, approached getting married. I didn't want to hurt John, but his persistence had such a negative effect on me that I even pleaded with my parents to let me change colleges. Dad's answer was a definite no, but my adult eyes were beginning to open: No way would I spend my life on a farm (or any place) with a guy whose manipulative ways left me cold.

Meeting college students and making friends from other parts of the United States, traveling and working in summer resorts, plus an eye-opening geography class that signaled another world beyond the Northwest, I knew that life was full of promise. I didn't plan on missing out!

4

The Youngest Son

Our youngest son, Tom, was a cuddly, affectionate baby and a busy toddler. He had a shorter attention span than his brothers five and seven years his senior. When I'd stick him in the playpen with his favorite soft toys while I tended to chores, his built-in timer lasted about twenty-five minutes. With less than five minutes to go, he'd be shoving a rattle through the slats or tossing his dog-eared teddy over the side. In two minutes he'd be hanging onto the edge in a standing position with all his toys on the floor, his grunts pushing towards a full-blown howl. To give myself an extra ten, I'd turn on John Phillip Sousa or Chubby Checker and move Tom to the portable jumper that was clamped and suspended from the kitchen door frame. He'd start out rocking and move on to a good roll. When his bounce became a kangaroo hop, I'd call it quits and try a new tack. If it was close to nap time, I'd stick him in the basket attached to the front of my bike and take him for a short ride around the block or until his head began to nod, then back home I'd race, pop him into bed, and hope nap time would be tranquil for both of us.

Now in his forties, Tom is still a mover, getting twice as much into a day as most people his age. His brothers used his position in the family to goad him into reacting. Tom would respond with gusto—a return punch, a fist poke below the shoulder, or an I'll-get-even-with-you face. Most of their teasing was good-natured, but when Tom was a preschooler, some of the name-calling had a thorny edge.

Tom liked to talk and he could drown out the best of them, which often resulted in his being picked on or given nicknames by the older boys—names like "motor-mouth", "hyper-diaper", and "Tommy Tittlemouse."

Doug's favorite ploy was to tell him, "You were supposed to be a girl, Tommy!"

"Tommy was supposed to be exactly like he is," I'd say indignantly. "A perfect little brother!"

As a first grader at Edgewood Elementary School in Eugene, Tom took part in a three-year experimental program in the arts. Edgewood was one of six grade schools in the US, at that time, to be awarded a million dollars for an arts enrichment program. Poets, pianists, string quartets, writers/playwrights, dramatists—even the Bella Lewitzky dance troupe—rotated between the schools every few months. Along with the normal primary school curriculum, this first-hand exposure to three solid years of so many art forms had, in my view, a lasting effect on Tom's confidence, versatility, and relationships with people, as well as his appreciation for all kinds of music, theater, and visual arts.

One specific and lasting result from those years was that Tom learned to play the double bass viol. He began playing when the instrument was almost twice his size. In England he played bass in the Bottisham School Orchestra, then later in the Orchestra at Sheldon High School. In college he was recruited by his professor, Ingrid Weatherhead, to play in a local Chamber Group.

Tom played in several Eugene outdoor summer musicals during his student years and afterward was the bassist with a Chicago-style jazz group, "Henry and the Ham Hawks." The group had paying gigs at The Electric Station and other Eugene hot spots. When I watched him move in sync with his bass, his long, lean body swaying with the music, his heavy, endearing, Norwegian eyebrows that reminded me of Wes and his great-grandfather, his oval face intent on a Muddy Waters or a Howlin' Wolf tune, I'd admire the high-spirited young man he'd become. Tom's bass is long gone, but the confidence he gained from performing during those years still shows.

I started Tom skiing when he was four. It wasn't long before he'd caught up with the older kids, and I was the laggard. He played Little League baseball and, like his brothers, was good at individual sports—swimming, water skiing, tennis, and snow skiing. All three of our sons were late to mature, so except for high school soccer, the typical team sports were out for Tom. Fishing pole in hand, though, the patient side of his nature showed up early on.

With Wes or sometimes David at his side, Tom learned to read the water and catch trout on the fly. Not long ago, Tom and Wes were on a stream fishing trip in the Coast Range.

"I was surprised that Tom knew every logging road and fishing hole in the area," Wes said when they returned. "I asked him how come?"

"What do you think I did in college?" Tom had replied.

My cane had become a permanent appendage when twenty-year-old Tom asked me to go with him to hear Robert Cray at the University of Oregon's EMU one Saturday night. Few young people would care to be seen at a campus jazz concert with their mother, especially a gimp.

"Robert Cray is from Tacoma. He's great on guitar and vocals," Tom said. "How about coming with me?"

"It'll be late for me," I said, feeling flattered by the invitation but having more than a few negative feelings about an auditorium full of amplified music and undulating kids. "You know how tired I get."

"We'll go early and leave when you want. I can get a hand stamp and go back later."

Tom left his Volkswagen Jetta hatchback idling while he walked me by a few kids wearing those black-on-white *Frankie say RELAX* tee shirts. They slinked backwards into the dusk and the dense bushes close to the building's back door at our approach.

"Stay right here, Mom. I'll be back in a sec," he said with the authority of a campus cop, looking directly at the kids who were reeking of marijuana. Within minutes he had opened the back door to a room packed with college students wearing neon pink and shiny black, with big frizzed hair, headbands, and dangly earrings, all swaying to the sound of *Don't Be Afraid of the Dark*. I wasn't, but it was.

My protector even managed to bring me the only chair I saw in the entire place. Then he gave me a standing boost and told me to hang onto his shoulder so I could see over the moving throng to the raised platform where Cray, his drummer, and keyboard player were going full tilt, making great music. The sociologist in me remembers a room full of sinuous, probably sedated dancers, prompted by the music and the enthusiasm of youth.

Besides his inborn traits, Tom's sensitivity and broad interests were sharpened in three ways. Firstly, by that infusion of art at Edgewood Elementary. Secondly, by exploring England with me. Tom and I took advantage of every Bank Holiday Monday and any other free days that didn't coincide with the Americans' work week at the Lakenheath Base, where Wes practiced and the older boys went to school. Together we day-tripped to see interesting sights within a two-hour drive or train ride—Stratford-on-Avon, the theater in London, East Anglia's castles like Orford overlooking the sea, great house gardens and collections, which I made sure to keep short to match a pre-teen's attention span. Tom was game for any new experience.

Thirdly, by having been around me from the beginning of my MS onset. It was obvious to me that something was wrong with me at least a year before I was diagnosed. Tom was often there when I tripped and sometimes fell, squatted and couldn't get back up, dropped things, or barely made it to the closest loo without wetting my pants. Young Tom's unspoken empathy to my needs back then still seems unusual for a twelve-year-old. He took the changes in my stamina and abilities in stride, often helping without being asked—carrying groceries from the car, doing kitchen chores, even cooking, which today is a permanent hobby.

Today, Tom's wife, Cathy, says he is an exemplary husband. He's a hands-on father to his daughter, Lauren, taking her fishing, skiing, teaching her how to cook with flair, and passing on his enthusiasm for entertaining, gardening, and just plain having fun. He still approaches new experiences with gusto, including tent-camping on summer weekends and fishing and hiking with family and friends in places similar to the ones he loved as a kid.

Still, Wes or I know that when and if we need him, Tom will be right with us at the drop of a hat.

Tom and Cathy, 1997

5

An Awakening

In the early-1980s I sat in on a motivational seminar in downtown Seattle given for Peacehealth (then Health & Hospital Services) executives and their spouses. The seminar's content had shades of Norman Vincent Peale's book, "The Power of Positive Thinking." The instructor, Lou Tice, was a square, hulky, former football coach with a '50s butch. In spite of my distaste for his rah-rah approach, I took home an important conclusion: Decide what you want to do in life and then go for it. Write down your goals. Focus on them. Don't get sidetracked by stuff you have no control over.

When Tice made a point with his frequent male-oriented sports analogies, I had some trouble connecting. He did hit home when he said, "You are upset when you see a long-haired kid on the street, filthy dirty, cussing loudly, and smoking a cigarette. Forget it. Don't spend your energy worrying about things you have no control over. Take on the ones you do." Tice's advice was firmly grounded.

I wouldn't say I became more goal-oriented after Tice's seminar, but I thought a lot more about where I might direct my energies to help strengthen my weakened physical abilities and improve my present circumstances. I had encouraged my parents to move to Eugene in their last years. Our son Tom's choice of the U of O for college wasn't just lucky, it was a godsend (he was near enough to help when we needed him most). My decision to get involved in writing workshops and classes resulted in meeting like-minded and varied people.

In my mid-forties, before my cane became a near-permanent appendage to my right arm, Wes planned a trip for us that combined a medical meeting with a visit to his favorite cousin, Jack Thellman. Wes reserved a room at the Hyatt in downtown Kansas City where the conference was being held. He hoped to spend as much time as possible with Jack, who was in the advanced stages of prostate cancer.

More than two decades before, I'd driven across the country with friends. We'd avoided driving through major cities, and I remembered the entire Midwest as being flat and boring. I had no idea of the size of the twin Kansas Cities. I was looking forward to meeting Jack and his family but was nervous about what lay in store for me, both on this trip and in my future life.

Back then, one would have needed a gambler's sixth sense to know what I wanted from others. I wasn't even sure, myself! I was having trouble adjusting to living with MS in my own setting, so being around new relatives and strangers would be a challenge, especially since my modus operandi was part denial, part trial and error, and a big dose of naiveté. I hadn't yet accepted the fact that I couldn't always count on being able to walk a short block unassisted, climb more than two flights of stairs, or stand upright and safely hold a baby. Truth be known, I was still embarrassed by my handicap.

"I don't need a wheelchair to get to the plane," I told Wes. "I can manage my own carry-on!"

In those early years, traveling together was almost as demanding for Wes as it was for me. I tried to swallow my annoyance when the flight attendant stopped by our seats to confirm the wheelchair Wes had ordered for our arrival in Kansas City. He thanked her without looking at my stony face. But as I watched him wrestle with our bags in the overhead bin, my frustration turned to regret when I realized there was no way I could have managed my bag on my own. Wes deserved a reward for his patience, cautious preparations, and well-bitten tongue.

When Jack's wife, Janet met us at the arrivals area, I'd come to another realization: My preoccupation with maintaining my independence was making life harder for both of us. Without the wheelchair, I couldn't possibly have made it from the door of the plane to baggage claim, let alone to Janet's car.

Janet had a charming drawl. She didn't sound patronizing when she spoke (albeit nonstop): "Hon, you sit in front. Wes has been here before. Jack is expecting us to take a little sight-seeing detour and swing by your hotel on the way home so ya-all can check in and get comfy."

I'd imagined Kansas would be similar to the desert area between Bend and Burns in the springtime, but the drive from the airport through Overland Park to their house looked like Andrew Wyeth country—a surprise of rolling-green hills and grassy knolls, drives lined with beech, oak, maple, and walnut, and spacious, well-groomed yards.

Janet drove by their Presbyterian Church, which claimed a membership of three thousand. I'd heard the Midwest was ripe with churchgoers, but learning about so many in one place made me think of the Easter crowds in Vatican Square that I'd seen on TV.

The Brookside neighborhood she took us by overflowed with English-style architecture, looking like the quaint little shops I'd seen in Newmarket and Cambridge when we lived in England.

"Ya-all are lucky to be stayin' at our city's finest," she said as she pulled into the downtown Hyatt's guest loading. "Hallmark headquarters is right here at the Crown Center. While Wes is busy, there are superstores, boutiques, and restaurants all over the place. You'll love it!" Four enclosed floors of specialty shops had never been on my agenda, and having MS made my low tolerance for malls less than zero.

"I wouldn't mind a rest for a few hours," I said. "Why don't you two visit with Jack, and come by for me later?"

Thumbing through the booklet of hotel activities, I saw that the Crown Center shopping experience was described as quiet and relaxing. *Relaxing?* I decided to see if my mental picture of Midwesterners as unhurried, easygoing and polite held true—plus, I wanted to see how I made out among strangers and to test my physical ability alone.

The long hall from the hotel lobby to the Center was lined with enclosed glass windows. The displays were of Nordstrom-type women's clothes, elaborate china place settings, and children's clothing that only a grandmother would consider buying. I found myself stopping with an elbow or arm toward the wall, not to admire the display cases, but to check my strength and try to judge when I'd need to turn back. Beyond loomed the longest, steepest, fastest escalator I'd ever seen, with a landing at the top and then a second escalator. I had visions of every single member of Janet's church lining up behind me, ready to elbow me if necessary: men in three-piece suits with fat leather briefcases; women with spike-heeled shoes that clicked across the marble floors like timers. I stood to one side of the escalator, pretending to look for someone. Call it panic or paranoia, my anxiety got the best of me. The task of getting both feet on the first step without losing my balance was daunting. I imagined every passing person giving me a dirty look—*Move out of the way, lady. We're in a hurry!* I gave up on the escalator and couldn't get back to the safety of our room fast enough.

That night at dinner, Jack sat at the head of our table of nine. He was smiling, though muted—a fraction of the man I'd seen in their Christmas card pictures. It was evident that illness was overtaking his body. Jack and Janet, plus their three sons and daughters-in-law, fit my idea of soft-spoken, laid-back Midwesterners. They were playful with each other and couldn't have been more considerate of Wes and me. I felt relaxed around them and felt less self-conscious about my weakness.

"Have you had a chance to check out the Crown Center shops?" Jack asked.

"I'm saving that for tomorrow," I said.

When Wes went to the conference the following day, I settled into our room to read "A Sensible Life" by Mary Wesley. Like Flora in the novel, I yearned for the routine pleasures I'd formerly taken for granted—even a carefree walk through a shopping mall. Like Wesley's heroine, I wanted to appear sensible in my new life laced with fewer constraints. I also had time to think about the huge thanks I owed to Jack and Janet for opening their home to us with little fanfare during a terribly difficult time for them.

Seeing Jack live daily with a life-threatening cancer made me realize that my physical challenges were less daunting and that I had plenty to work on, beginning with my attitude. I resolved to try harder to pace myself, to save my energy for the important stuff in life, beginning with my immediate family. Accepting what each day offered me was a lot harder then than it is today.

And I've learned that what Garrison Keillor says is true: "The advantage of age, a few details stand for the whole…"

6

Water, My Balancing Act

In a 2009 interview with TIME magazine, the actor and stem-cell research advocate Michael J. Fox was asked how he remained optimistic in difficult circumstances. He said he had no choice about whether he had Parkinson's, but he had nothing but choices about how he reacted to it. "I think it's about acceptance," Fox said.

MS causes the body's immune system to attack itself, resulting in a range of ailments from mild muscle weakness to complete paralysis. The side effects of my MS have stabilized over a period of more than thirty years. After the sudden onset I experienced in 1978, the rest of my symptoms developed gradually. The damage to my central nervous system and the resulting weaknesses remain in my lower body, affecting my ability to walk, my balance, and most frustratingly, my energy level.

I was (and still am) determined not to let my disease define me. After several years and many setbacks, I accepted what I call the shortcomings associated with my symptoms and began to search for fulfilling ways to spend my days. Since my physical life had become circumscribed, I tried to sharpen my mental acuity by seeking out new and challenging skills.

I grew up in Washington, near the confluence of the Columbia and Cowlitz Rivers, with a man-made lake in the center of town. My parents oriented their leisure towards the ocean, the rivers, and nearby lakes. I became blessed with an inherent love of the outdoors and any activities involving water.

Dad said he threw me in Spirit Lake, Washington, when I was three, and I took off swimming. I don't remember having proper lessons until lifesaving and water ballet in high school and college (unless you count Dad's summer crawl, breaststroke, backstroke demonstrations), so maybe he was telling the truth. As a family we tent-camped at Spirit Lake for a number of years and then rented a bare-bones, rustic cabin next to the creek at the base of Harmony Falls, with Mt. St. Helens still intact as a backdrop across the lake.

In the early years following my diagnosis, I was determined to keep myself fit. Since walking any distance appeared unlikely, it seemed natural to begin my fitness regime with swimming and water-related exercise options that had always been a part of my life. I also read about a disabled skiing class in the Eugene Parks and Recreation winter catalogue. *Whoopee!* It involved six day trips to Willamette Pass with a busload of special-needs kids, plus Ryan, my very own volunteer from the University of Oregon. But as I sat next to Ryan that first frigid January morning with the bus windows so steamy that the gray daylight couldn't possibly have filtered through and with a bunch of noisy, runny-nosed kids, I had the opposite of an adrenaline rush.

"With your experience," Ryan said, "Using these Canadian crutches with little skis attached should be a breeze."

The breeze lasted until we reached the top of the bunny hill. I slid off the lift well enough and then stopped on the flat so Ryan could strap the ski- crutches on my arms. After that I proceeded to land on my rear going over the first downhill bump.

"You know," I said, feeling like a quitter before I'd even begun, "I'm going to share you with one of the kids who need you a lot more than me. I'll hang out in the coffee shop until time to go home. Just help me get these cotton-picking weights off my arms so I can ski down pole-less." Like a bicyclist riding without handlebars, I made it to the bottom, followed by Ryan who wanted to make sure I was OK. *OK? Not really*—just a baby step closer to being realistic about my limitations. I'd skied enough years to manage the bunny hills without poles, but it was obvious that if I fell down it would be impossible to get back up again.

Success was sweeter the following spring when I joined a Parks and Recreation beginning sailing class. There were twelve people in the class, two partners to each small boat with a mainsail and jib. Martha, my partner, was a hefty redhead who knew starboard from port and the right-of-way rules. It helped that she took the helm on our first sortie into Dexter Lake, and kept us from hitting another boat of fledgling learners when we came about. I became skilled at ducking under the mast. When it was my turn to push the tiller, I yelled "Ready about," and felt a tingling sense of freedom moving with the bubbling water at my side and a quiet breeze on my face. Our final test together came on day six. We were to tip the sail boat over and then right it again. My love of cold plus my built-in water-wings did me justice that day, as I splashed into the chilly lake near the stern. Martha wasn't so keen about getting wet. She slithered in on the same side but nearer the bow. With her strong arms and loud bark (giving me directions), we were righted before I could say Jack Robinson.

Much as I enjoyed my brief exposure to sailing, it became clear that home-based workouts were best for me. For the past thirty years stationary bicycling, ski-walking (sliding) in the event I can find snow, and water exercise have become my most valued workout activities. When

I'm in the water I feel relaxed, refreshed, and for a time, almost like the Dolphin synchronized swimmer I had been in high school. My five- or six-days-a-week routine of laps, stretches, and deep-water walking with the aid of Styrofoam barbells and a flotation belt has kept me mostly upright and sane—physically, and I might even say emotionally! Water is my saving grace.

And I've been lucky. When we returned after living in England for three years, we bought a house in Eugene that was next door to the most generous neighbors imaginable, who happened to have a backyard swimming pool. Paula was one of the first to call after we moved in. She brought flowers, a bottle of wine, and a caring offer for me to use their pool during the summer. Weekday mornings were the time that worked best—for her family's privacy and my need to limber up early in the day. Six-year-old Heather was often in the pool alongside me, making fun and games out of what was (and still is) the most redeeming activity in my life. I also swam and exercised at the Sheldon High School pool three or more days a week, feeling quite martyr-ish in winter. I chose mornings, when the diving pool was relatively empty. Getting in the car and driving to Sheldon, getting dressed and showered, and then returning home in the rain wasn't half as much fun as popping over to Paula's on my scooter, but it was an essential part of the balancing act that helped me keep moving.

In 1986 I saw Dr. Bruce Becker, a senior associate with Rehabilitation Medicine in Eugene/Springfield, who prescribed a twice-weekly water fitness routine for me under the supervision of his partner, Dick Brown, the former coach of Olympic runner and gold-medalist Mary Slaney. Brown and Dr. Becker formed a company named Sci-Ex—for science and deep-water exercise. At that time the building across from Sacred Heart Hospital housed two Sci-Ex water tanks called Aqua Arks—five feet wide, eight feet long, and seven feet deep.

It was heady to find myself in a tank next to Mary Slaney or some other athlete who was training in the water using the newly developed flotation system for healing tendons, joints, or sore backs. After a lifetime in athletics, Brown told a Register Guard reporter that he found tremendous gratification working with non-sports clients as well as athletes in water-therapy treatment. His clients included people recovering from accidents and operations, and those, like me, with multiple sclerosis.

"These people are like athletes," Brown said. "They have potential and goals, just as athletes do. I enjoy, and always have, seeing people get the most out of their potential."

World-class athlete, Jimmie Heuga, who placed third in the slalom at the 1964 Winter Olympics, didn't give up after being diagnosed with MS. In 1970 he established the Heuga Center for the treatment of MS in Vail, Colorado. As his disease progressed Jimmie could be seen doing snow plow turns by the beginner's chair lift at Beaver Creek near Vail, wearing laminated fiberglass leg supports on his thighs and calves. Huega's perseverance might even be called a Calvinist's form of Divine Grace. The motto of the Heuga

Patty exercising with barbells

Center is "Learn to make do with what you have left." His example has helped many people with MS, and I would guess many others, like myself, who have read about his work and have the determination not to let adversity get the best of us.

The Pacific Northwest is the platform that launched me, having been born in the shadow of the Cascades and living close to the Pacific Ocean most of my life. I've written of my early years in Longview, Washington, through the time of my marriage at twenty-two. Those treasured memories of family and friends all seem to center around my sense of place: my first summer job at Spirit Lake when I was seventeen; the two summers before my freshman and sophomore years at OSU when I worked at Lake Quinault

Lodge in the Olympic National Forest; and the summer before my senior year in college, when I worked in Ocean City, Maryland, picking up a travel bug that hangs around incessantly in spite of my disability.

No wonder I feel like I'm part fish. If Dad actually did throw me into Spirit Lake at a tender age, I'm grateful to him that, in his own way, he pushed me to love the water. Today I call my water-exercise routine my saving grace.

My mother's faith, unconditional love, and trust in my ability to cope with adversity and the difficulties in my later life help me still. She's in my daily thoughts as I continue to work at pacing and compromise.

I'm grateful to both my parents for giving me my love of being in the woods—to smell pine, cedar, and fir bows after a light rain or watch a Great Blue Heron long and quietly enough to see him spear and swallow his dinner in one fell swoop or paddle my kayak across a lake with strokes so soft that even a bashful beaver might give me a nod before slapping the water to disappear.

As far as today's challenges go, you'll still find me still in the driver's seat, working on my goals, and mostly upright—unless, of course, I'm napping.

7

Esprit

Adventure and romance are awash in a paradise where emerald volcanic peaks soar above vivid blue and green lagoons teaming with multicolored fish, where orchids, gardenias, hibiscus, and frangipani grow wild, and where Tahitian fishermen paddle outrigger canoes into a melodramatic reddish-orange sunset.

"How about joining us for two weeks in French Polynesia with the Andersons and Hills?" George said to Wes. "Eight days on a 50-foot trimaran with private staterooms. We'll sail to Bora Bora to snorkel in the famous lagoon. Then we'll cap if off with a stay in your own private thatched-roof hut with steps into the sea at the Bali Hai on Moorea."

"Whoa! Let me check with the boss," Wes said.

After reading the brochure and listening to George, the invitation was a clincher.

We were on our way to paradise. Never mind the eight-hour wait at LAX, not to mention being jammed for the next eleven in the middle-back row of an Air France DC 10, our knees hugging our chests.

"Isn't this great?" George said, standing in the aisle with a travel-agent's bravado and a stab of First Class snobbishness.

"The food and wine aren't bad, and the close proximity to the john works until you have to crawl over three pairs of reluctant knees, step on toes, and pray you'll get there clean and dry," Wes said, our seat mates nodding in agreement. "Slumming, are you?"

"Just wait," George said. "The two weeks ahead will be perfect."

Except for George and Nicki, our group felt a bit like exhausted refugees when we landed at Papeete's airport at 7:00 a.m. (PST). We stuffed our duffle bags into two luggage carriers with me and my cane atop one, hanging onto the basket like it was a roller-coaster seat, and off we headed for our Air Tahiti transfer to the Leeward Isle of Huahine.

When our eight-passenger plane landed on a dirt runway that looked more like a Junior High track than a landing strip with only three people standing in the doorway of the small thatched-roof terminal hut, I realized that at least my dream of being cut off from the real world for a few days had begun.

A cabby drove us to a perfect, white-sand-edged bay where our Captain, Dave, was waiting by the Zodiac to transfer us to his moored yacht, Esprit.

Andersons, Hansons and Hills behind Patty and Wes

Aboard, and as oriented as our lack of sleep allowed, Dave set about in the galley fixing a great lunch of fresh pineapple, pamplemousse (grapefruit), banana bread, and a mahi mahi caught that morning. The eight of us donned our bathing suits, squeezed our duffels under our stateroom beds, and headed for the deck to sun, snooze, then lazily swim to shore and back. Given the empty beach, the crystal-clear water, and the warmth of the sun, nothing, not even a bit of rain, could have marred the tranquility I felt knowing eight full and lovely days of sailing were ahead.

The second day we motored along Huahine's uneven coastline, past dammed lagoons where traditional-style fish traps were still being used. We anchored near the village of Maeva to explore the ancient marae (Polynesian temples containing a stone altar for religious ceremonies). I could almost see those distant Polynesians setting sail in their outriggers, off to explore the Pacific Ocean and spread their culture to Hawaii and beyond.

Another swim and snorkel, and then we made a breezy sail to our anchoring spot for the night, in the island lagoon that Tahaa shares with Raiatea.

"The ship's real chef, Hinano, will meet us tomorrow on Raiatea. She'll show you the secrets of our most sacred island, take over the galley, and serve up her Tahitian poi (banana, papaya, pineapple and tapioca mashed together and baked in banana leaves) topped with fresh coconut milk," Dave said, obviously relieved to cede his wilting cook's hat.

We'd barely finished dinner when the rains came on with typhoon density.

"Kendall, give me a hand with the tarpaulin up here. Ladies, shut the portholes in your rooms. Guys, I'll need you to help stow the gear. Looks like we're in for a big one," Dave barked. "We need to head for the moorings marina at Uturoa, (largest city on Raiatea) and tie up until the storm passes."

We were in for one of the heaviest, most prolonged storms in Polynesia's recorded history. Three feet of rain in two days and winds were up to 80 knots. Our soggy band of amazingly upbeat Oregonians took refuge inside the Esprit at the marina moorage, only venturing out to watch other boats struggle to return through the raging sea with torn and shredded sails.

Except for plenty of pamplemousse, bananas, and

coffee, Dave was out of food supplies and open to any sustenance suggestions, physical or mental. His girlfriend, Hinano, was going to have a tough time joining us. He fished ten slickers out of the hold and begrudgingly led Marita, Nicki, Joyce, and Kendall to the grocery store to load up on spaghetti and canned chicken before those supplies were depleted by the hordes of other stranded sailors.

For three days we sat in the cabin next to the galley playing gin rummy by the hour, laughed at stupid second-grade jokes, and wrote and told stories to amuse ourselves. Kendall's yarn won the prize for the most creative:

> Our group responded to the flooding and resultant havoc to the inhabitants of Raiatea by setting up the Raiatea Emergency Ambulatory Clinic, which became affectionately known as REAK. During the course of this operation Dr. Hanson successfully delivered three babies. One mother was saved from surgical intervention when Dr. Hanson ingeniously fashioned outlet forceps using 2 salad spoons from the galley of the Esprit.
> Dr. Hills set up a outpatient clinic. He opened several boils, and treated many traumatic wounds. He was credited with saving the leg of a diabetic fisherman. Dr. Anderson successfully treated many cases of dengue fever and malaria, but his biggest

contribution was preventing an outbreak of the plague by developing a protocol for effective rodent control following the flooding.

Dr. Jacobs, of course, administered the entire operation flawlessly and developed such close rapport with the village leaders that he was offered one million Polynesian Francs per month and all the pamplemousse he could eat if he would stay on as the new administrator of the hospital in Uturoa.

The girls jumped into action and set up a soup kitchen to feed the hundreds made homeless by the deluge. They were so proficient and their food so well liked that the official dish of Raiatea was changed to spaghetti with meat sauce.

When the time came to leave our moorage, the villagers crowded the dock, some prostrating themselves on the wet planks in a symbolic expression of gratitude.

As the Esprit left the mooring, Captain Dave and his crew, Hinano, appeared on deck wearing the green and gold tee shirts given by the Oregon contingent. In honor of this gallant group, it is said that the Marina name will forevermore be known as Hug-a-Duck Harbor.

As we sailed into the lagoon at Bora Bora, the incomparable beauty that I had in my mind from the museum works of Gauguin, Maugham, and Michener seemed untouched, at least from a distance. Closer to the moorage we could see that the flooding had brought mud down the mountains into the sea, coloring the water a light milk-chocolate. No way was I going to step into that dirty water from our thatched-roof bungalow.

Fortunately, the seventeen-mile road ride circling the island was paved, and the driver of 'le truck' slowed enough through the mud puddles to keep us from getting sprayed light brown. He pointed out land crabs and fallen coconuts, avoided live chickens, and showed us where the American Base had been during WWII. The flowering and flaming colors I expected to see growing wild on the hillsides had been supplanted by limp fronds, sagging tree branches, and muddy ditches. Oh well, I'd seen enough those first two days to know that all would soon be well again in paradise.

My maroon duffle bag, a Sears sale item purchased before the trip, was damp all the way through from being stowed on the floor of our moist stateroom. I'd packed a new white denim skirt on the bottom to wear for dinners out on Bora Bora and Moorea. I didn't know whether to laugh or cry as I shook it out and saw the wavering rosy stripes down the middle, the back, and along the sides.

"Think tie-dye," Wes said. "It's an original!"

The entire trip was a first. The congeniality of the group—good humored, un-claustrophobic, and all able to "hang loose" in tense circumstances—made it memorable and fun. Best of all, there was not a single nursemaid in the bunch—the helper-types I'd needed most to avoid in my disease-conscious life back home.

In attempting to write about that trip to the most exotic place I've ever been, what hits me today is not the lush beauty of French Polynesia or of being in the worst rainstorm of my life or the comical ride on an airport luggage carrier. What strikes me is that I don't remember feeling disabled the entire two weeks, although I'd been diagnosed with MS nine years earlier. My weak bladder was nothing new. I had a fold-up cane, but I don't remember using it, and the walking and balancing that normally troubled me seemed simple with the handles that were situated throughout the yacht, both below and on deck.

Twenty-five years later, when we meet our friends from that resilient group and bring up the Polynesian odyssey that turned into such a lark, we laugh about the dollar Wes was charged for two olives in his martini on Bora Bora and the unnecessary guilt George felt, as if he were somehow directly responsible for the weather. When Dick and Wes sat on the deck that first night smoking cigars, the wind changed and the smoke blew into the open porthole of Nicki and George's stateroom.

"I can't stand that smell," Nicki told George.

"You have to," he'd said.

An exotic vacation? I wouldn't say so. A rainstorm in

Oregon has it all over that Tahitian deluge. But fun? Yes. It was one of the most memorable two weeks away we've had, and the company was incomparable.

8

Waiting and Thinking

"What if I'd never come? I asked myself. How could I bear never to have seen this?" —Nancy Mairs

In February 1983, I was alone in Tokyo's Narita Airport with a three hour layover. Though my MS had been diagnosed four years earlier, I was still suffering from denial, especially when my independence was involved. I had told Wes that I was perfectly capable of walking (and taking the available transportation) when the United Airlines plane from Taipei landed at the Tokyo airport and of getting myself to the Seattle gate.

In spite of my denial, Wes had ordered a wheelchair for me. Boy was I relieved when a Japanese porter met me at the door of the plane with a wheelchair and sign that said MRS. JACOBS. How stupid of me to even consider going it alone through a long concourse walk, an elevator ride, and a tram to the distant gate with rain pelting down like Oregon in November.

 Although the porter brought me to the Seattle gate's desk and close enough to the bathroom to be expedient, he wasn't about to part with the wheelchair. That left me with my over-sized carry-on (no rolling wheels back then) and a folded sectional travel cane to get around.

 "Leave wheel chair? Restaurant? Ladies room?" I asked him in the loud voice people use when they can't speak the language. I'd hoped to use the chair like a cart to lean on while roaming the airport. In view of my physical limitations, I was pretty sure I wouldn't be returning to Asia in the near future.

 The porter gave me a puzzled look and shook his head. "I return," he said with a part smile. I felt bewildered, and as naive as the newlyweds I'd left behind after our week together in Taiwan. Our twenty-five-year-old son, Doug, had just married a Chinese girl. Their improbable union worried me more than the difficulties I was having in navigating my return trip home. The porter did wheel me to the plane. The marriage did last ten years but no more.

 I got to Seattle in the early evening after thirty-some hours without sleep. My exhaustion was complete, and I was on the verge of tears, facing another incredibly long layover before my plane to Eugene left. This time I managed to snag one of those wheelchairs with iron rods behind the handles, high enough for a kid to use as balance bars. In healthier days, I would have tried to get an earlier flight home, but the thought of finding my way to the ticket counter behind a rickety wheelchair required more energy than I could muster. So I sat there waiting, thinking, and sifting through the rubble of my life, through the unpredictable twists and turns in our son Doug's makeup that led him to the life of an expatriate in Taiwan and his marriage to nineteen-year-old May Wu.

To say Doug was a daredevil as a kid is probably stretching the truth, but he did seem to have issues when it came to authoritarian edicts. Fortunately, I'm not aware of all the risks he took before he was twenty-one, when he left for Taipei to seek his fortune teaching English as a second language. But I knew about some of them.

When Doug was six, we lived in a rental on the corner of 4th and E Street in Lake Oswego. Tyron Creek was an undeveloped forested area of meandering trails through firs and cottonwoods. Several blocks from our house was a precarious tree swing over the stream. I often took the boys there on our walks.

"Don't come down here without me," I told Doug, who had permission to play with the neighbor kids across the street if their moms were home and he was welcome.

David was napping one afternoon when the doorbell rang. Doug stood there pasty white, supported by two older neighborhood boys. He had a huge bloody gash across his chest that left a permanent scar.

"You told me I couldn't go down there," he whispered, and then passed out.

When Doug was in college he had the gall to ask his dad for a loan to buy a Suzuki. Wes had seen many calamitous outcomes from motorcycle accidents in his emergency-room days, most involving young men. More than once Wes told all three of our sons, "Don't even think about owning one of the riskiest modes of transportation on the planet."

With "no" the obvious answer, Doug asked his grandfather to lend him the money for the motorcycle and drew another blank. Where he ultimately got the cash remains a mystery. But what happened to his brand new Suzuki within a week after purchase was no surprise. Doug was one lucky guy!

A woman in a "two-ton Yank tank" (British term for big American cars) backed out of her parking place at what used to be Albertsons on the corner of Oakway and Coburg Road in Eugene and didn't see Doug on his motorcycle. She whammed into him, totaling the Suzuki. Miracle of miracles, Doug was left unscathed.

After high school, Doug's impetuous nature and his search for new and challenging experiences seemed to control his educational choices. Had our country's academic track been similar to England's—students are locked into career decisions at an early age—his choice of OSU and Forestry his freshman year (Doug was on the Dean's list all three terms) might have given him a permanent vocation that matched his love of the outdoors. But we were still living in England. He had a knack for languages and a thirst for travel that landed him as a sophomore at the University of Maryland's branch in Munich, studying German, sightseeing exotic European cities on school outings (Prague, Paris, Vienna), and skiing in the Alps.

Back at OSU for his junior year, he decided to take Mandarin Chinese at Linn/Benton Community College. I'm sure Doug's Taiwanese teacher didn't have to do much talking to convince him that all he'd need to get a job teaching English in Taipei was a one-way ticket to that city plus her letter of recommendation. He was told there were plenty of places to live near the school, easy bus and train services, and lots of English-speaking young people. Doug was off—ready for adventures and to hunt his fortune.

When May Wu first walked into her English class in Taipei and took one look at the ruddy, curly-haired, reddish-blond teacher with blue eyes and a chin-dimpled grin, I'm sure she was intrigued. My guess is that she also envisioned Doug as a ticket to America should she win his favor over the other girls in class, who were undoubtedly of like minds.

When they began dating and then decided to marry, I imagine Doug had taken note of her family background. May's father, J. Ping Wu, had been a young physician in Chiang Kai-shek's Nationalist Party in 1949 when the Kuomintang fled to Taiwan to regroup and make plans to retake the mainland from Mao Zedong's Chinese Communist Party. Thirty-five years later Dr. Wu's loyalty, his holdings, and his connections to the leaders in present-day Taiwan (Republic of China) were substantial. With a wife, one son, and three daughters, his feet were firmly planted on Taiwanese soil.

As I sat on that unforgiving seat at SeaTac, I wondered and worried about how an individualist like Doug would find happiness should the couple decided to live permanently on an island about the size of Oregon with a population of 22 million and surrounded by May's family. Doug was positive he would be accepted as one of their own. Given the dichotomy of their backgrounds, I was skeptical.

My anxiety was well-founded. In a few short years May was pregnant and only wanted to leave Oregon and return home where she would be surrounded by a doting family and hired hands to wash diapers, cook, and relieve her from night feedings.

Had I kept notes from their wedding and the few days following, I could have filled a journal. Instead, I have snippets and memories of what happened a quarter of a century ago, jogged by a few formally posed pictures: May in tulle, satin, and netting dotted with seed pearls, her black hair and eyes made more prominent by the flowered hairpieces securing her waist-length veil; Doug looking very grave in a vested black suit, formal white-studded shirt, pocket hanky, and red bow tie holding white gloves—not the Doug I knew! The formal pictures were taken before the big day. He posed wearing white socks, but wore proper dark socks on the wedding day. Doug told me they were married three times—first in a civil ceremony required by law before we arrived, then a private Wu family ceremony, and finally the big event held in a large hotel ballroom.

In a private dining room the night before the wedding, the entire Wu family plus the three of us were treated to the same twelve-course dinner that would be served after the ceremony. On the wedding day the tables for ten were covered with white starched linen, centered by lazy-susan-type centerpieces for serving one course at a time and starting with Wes and me, May's father and mother, the groom and bride, and so on according to sex, age, and family status. A Chinese woman who owned the boarding house where Doug had lived in Taipei, whom he referred to as his *second mother*, stayed by my side during most of the festivities and served as my interpreter. When the fish course was served on a large platter—head, tail, fins and all—I asked second mother if I could pass it by with a "No, thank you."

"Just a small piece after your husband's helping is polite," she said. Feeling watched and nervous, that's all I cared to manage with my limited chop-stick-dexterity.

The tables in the hotel ballroom were divided on either side and down the middle by a portable white picket fence covered with pastel plastic flowers and ivy. After the guests were seated below, we parents (plus Wes' translator and May's brother-in-law) were up on a stage facing over two hundred guests. Doug and May came through the gate at the back of the hall and proceeded down the flower-edged aisle to the canned strains of Wagner's "Bridal Chorus." Their chairs were at center stage behind the microphone. As the first speaker, May's father gave his well-wishes (I was told) to the couple. Next came Wes with his speech prepared and read in English, translated sentence by sentence, with pauses for the audience to clap. Finally, in fluent Mandarin, Doug spoke of his respect for the Wu family and how happy he was to be marrying May.

At the head table I sat between Wes and Dr. Wu's most influential friend, General Wong, who spoke perfect Oxford English, making polite conversation and giving me the benefit of easy answers.

"Are you enjoying your stay in Taiwan?"

"Very much."

"Our weather in February can be dreary."

"Much like where we live in Oregon."

While the guests ate, we accompanied Doug, May, and her parents to toast at every single table in the entire room with the worst, beige-colored wine I'd ever tasted. I switched to tea. Obligation met.

It seemed like hours that we smiled, nodded, and toasted table after table of grinning faces who said, "How are you?" or "Happy wedding" or "Thank you, Thank you." I was exhausted, my face hurt, and I hoped to opt out of my last mother-of-the-groom responsibility, but that didn't happen. May stood beside me in a red velvet street-length dress and matching hair bows with her mother and Doug. We handed out baskets full of hard candy for the kids, boxed cigarette samples for the adults, and fielded more two-syllable questions in English plus "Thank you, Thank you." The guests tucked their gifts in the baskets—small, gold-etched, red envelopes containing money.

I should have returned home with Wes the day after the wedding. The few days of sightseeing in Taipei accompanied by May's mother, who didn't like sitting beside me because the only Chinese I knew was "xie, xie," added to my exhaustion and both of our nerves.

"Why does your mother like cows so much?" she asked Doug, when I kept pointing out water buffaloes grazing on either side of the roadway.

"Our cows are different in Oregon," he said, winking at me.

She was taken aback when I bought an umbrella at Taipei's Art Museum to take home as a gift. She looked at me like I was a nut case.

"She believes giving anyone an umbrella gift brings the recipient very bad luck," Doug said. The umbrella is still with me. I wasn't about to wish any bad fortune on a friend.

When I asked to stop at the market to buy one of the round, point-centered straw hats that I'd seen on Chinese people in pictures, Mrs. Wu had a hissy-fit.

"Why does she want a farmer's hat? Only farmers wear

those things!" After that she insisted on sitting in front with Doug and told May she should sit in the back seat until we got home.

Neither of the Wu's large homes—the one in Taoyuan, about forty-five minutes south of Taipei, nor the second in the hills beyond—was ostentatious. The furniture was sparse but seemed comfortable enough until I was finally left alone in a large, chilly bedroom with a fluffy European-style quilt. My body was talking to me, and that bed looked heavenly—until I pulled back the quilt to find a hard plank covered by a single sheet. With a lump in my throat the size of a prune, I called to Doug to find me another blanket and bring me a pair of his socks. I lay down on top of the quilt dressed in flannel pajamas and a long-sleeved wool sweater, with the second quilt and my raincoat over all, and finally slept.

As I sat in the airport waiting area feeling vulnerable and exhausted, I couldn't help but wonder about the similarities in our personalities that had caused me to insist on traveling alone in my rather fragile state. Doug's unpredictability had led him into a life I couldn't have imagined for him as a youngster or even an unconventional teenager. His independent nature gave me cause to worry about how he would fit into the close-knit Wu family. As a teenager Doug would jump from a cliff into an unknown pool near our campsite. Like him, I would swim in the ocean without fear, even after I had MS and my legs had become weak. During the trip to Taiwan, I was still experimenting with my strengths and weaknesses—a disabled woman who had always loved traveling. I hadn't acknowledged that a few days of rest after a strenuous and fatiguing time would allow me to resume normal activity for my condition—being able to slowly walk for 50 yards, do 30 minutes of vigorous water exercise, and have an active day that ended in a good eight hours of sleep. Having overdone it after the wedding, it took the better part of a week at home for me to feel the way I'd come to expect. I was certain my condition had exacerbated. Now I'm in my seventies (with what Wes calls my cavalier approach to my disability) and still searching for new adventures.

Doug and May spent eight years together and produced two lovely daughters. After Doug's divorce and return to Eugene in 1991, he moved into our two-bedroom condo, set up his computer, and began job-searching. Networking became a major dinnertime topic. Through mutual friends and acquaintances, he had several opportunities in Seattle and San Francisco, but after living in a crowded country halfway around the world for a decade, Doug knew the big city wasn't for him. He wanted to live and work in Oregon, around the people and places he'd known in his younger years. He wanted to spend time pursuing the outdoor activities he'd missed while living in Taiwan.

Not long after his homecoming, my regrettable choice

of the Robin Williams movie, "Mrs. Doubtfire," made it obvious how much Doug missed Esther and Micki, and most likely their mother as well. He got teary, stood up, and headed for bed saying, "I can't watch the rest of this."

For Wes and me, having our granddaughters spend many long summer days and weeks with us at our lake house every year gave us the wonderful feeling of what it was like to have our own girls. Being a part of two such different cultures must have played a role in their unbridled enthusiasm and curiosity for any and all experiences. Wes gave them patient and hands-on cooking lessons. They followed me into the garden with hand trowels, picked huckleberries for our breakfast pancakes, looked for edible mushrooms in the woods with me, and bickered over whose turn it was to ride on the front or back of my scooter on the trails around our property and close by.

Doug would arrive to visit us after a night of tent camping with the girls at Hills Creek Reservoir or Archie Knowles Creek. Alone with their dad, they roasted hot dogs and marshmallows, caught crawdads, and saw the constellations clearer than at any time in their lives. At the lake and nearby ocean, Doug taught them to discover and experience the many water activities he loved as a kid.

But best of all for me, those two girls seemed to have the sensitivity and watchful eyes of trained therapists (the truth be told). An arm was always ready for me to grab onto at a railingless step, an offer was always there to run into the store, hands were ever present to clear the table.

Thanks to Doug's return home, all four of our lives were enriched in countless ways, and not a single one of us will forget it.

9

Fur and Choices

"Fashion can be bought. Style, one must possess." —Edna Woolman Chase.

The last time the black seal-fur coat and hat, which is tucked away inside an air-tight bag in the corner of our guestroom closet, saw the light of day was twelve years ago. My fashionable, nearly six-foot tall and slim daughter-in-law wore the coat with the cuffs turned down and without objection to the Christmas Eve service at the Presbyterian Church of the Siuslaw. Cathy was the most elegantly attired person in that small sanctuary, and I'm quite sure that none of the turned heads in church (or anywhere else in Florence, Oregon, for that matter) had animal rights on their minds. I thought of giving Cathy the coat long ago, but she lives in a suburb of Portland, and wearing fur anywhere in Western Oregon except for the coastal town of Florence could be suicidal. I have no reason to think that PETA (People for the Ethical Treatment of Animals) suspect me of harboring an ancient seal pelt or plan to come knocking on my door anytime soon. If by some quirk that should happen, I'd spin a true yarn that might quell any protests.

Originally full length, the seal coat bears the signature and taste of my Uncle Austil's third wife, Larissa, a white-Russian former dance and language teacher at the University of Hawaii. As a child during the Revolution, Larissa fled Russia with her family, coming to California via Europe, and then moving on to Honolulu. I never met my uncle's "Mad Russian beauty" during the ten years they were together, but I did see several cork-sized holes in the grass-cloth walls of his hillside home on Oahu. This leads me to believe Mother's stories about popping champagne corks, trays of caviar, and Russian vodka flowing at the wild parties that Austil and Larissa threw for the visiting officers of Russian ships in port.

Mother in her seal jacket

Mother's disapproval of my uncle's lifestyle didn't keep her from accepting the fur as a gift from Larissa when she and my dad visited their home in Honolulu or having Teply's in Portland alter it into a three-quarter coat with matching muff and hat.

"You needn't feel guilty about wearing it, Mom," I told her. "The Russian trapper that harpooned that seal over a hundred years ago would have eaten the meat, lit his lamps with the oil, and used the fur he didn't sell to wear during the freezing winter."

"I wish you hadn't said that," she said. "I don't like thinking about my new jacket that way."

Having overcome her mild objections, Mother looked gracefully stylish wearing the jacket, standing between Governors Evans and Hatfield in the 1965 opening of the Longview-Rainier Bridge. My Grandfather Vandercook was the chief engineer of the crew that built the toll bridge between Washington and Oregon near the Port of Longview. Grandfather had died twelve years earlier, and Grandmother was housebound, so Mother was chosen to represent the family at the ribbon cutting.

I tried to talk Esther, my eldest granddaughter, into making Mother's mink stole into a vest during her high school sewing class.

"Gross, Grandma!" she said. "Cut up and wear a helpless animal raised in a cage? No way!"

I didn't mention that as a youngster Esther had loved playing with the seal muff. She even slept with it on occasion.

A year or so ago I decided it might be best to use Mother's fur coat and stole as tax-deductible gifts to a local theaters. After the younger women in my family had rejected both the furs, I found that those wraps had lost their allure for me—in spite of Larissa's renowned sense of style.

Blondes have more fun.

In my thirties I had my hair frosted, sang loudly in the shower, and bought a thick-collared rabbit-fur jacket off the sale rack at Kaufman's downtown store. Every other winter weekend our family skied at Mt. Bachelor. Once a year, Wes and I drove to Sun Valley, Idaho, with two other couples with whom we shared a two-bedroom, one bathroom suite at the Tamarack Motel in Ketchum. The small living room had a fold-down sofa. We flipped a coin to see which couples got the bedrooms, switching mid-week when the sheets were changed. Bathroom tenure was limited by six bodies, and we all skied so hard every day that I wasn't inclined to do much singing in the shower. But out on the town at night, I remember feeling like a million-dollar, après-ski Theresa Brewer in my fluffy, dense-fur jacket. It may not have been in fashion, but it sure fit my style.

The coat was a speckled cream color, with vertical pelts of beige over the bust and sleeves and lining the downy-soft collar. Thoughts of PETA didn't exist in my mind back then, but for some reason (inhibition, maybe?) I don't remember wearing my favorite jacket in Eugene. The chilly winters in laid-back Bend, Oregon, gave me good reason to don it often, and I did. I'd already gotten more than my money's worth when I packed the jacket off to England for three years of breath-raising winters and yearly ski trips to the European Alps with our three sons.

Preparing to return to the States from England in the spring of 1978, I trudged to the Lakenheath Base Thrift

Shop to consign my beloved rabbit jacket along with all the other goods we would no longer need back in Eugene. I hung my jacket on the coat rack with a twenty-five dollar price tag hooked onto the sleeve and scoured the room to see which young woman would be lucky enough to snap it up and have even a few of the good times I associated with it. Parting with that coat was rather like saying goodbye to a good friend—one I knew I wouldn't see again. My recent MS diagnosis meant that my days on the ski slopes were over. That day I felt as if I was leaving behind my former self and a pleasure-filled life.

    My rabbit jacket came to mind again when we were staying at Rancho Jacona in northern New Mexico, near Santa Fe, Los Alamos, and the Sangre de Cristo Mountains. Instead of gazing at the view and lush grounds near our rented casita, I found myself drawn to the fenced rabbit warren on the property, hoping not to see a bunny with cream-colored fur sprinkled with beige. Today I might be called a PETA-minded person, troubled by the Rancho's resident house cats that lurk behind the fence, stalking the peep-holes and crawl spaces in the dry, uneven mounds of dirt. I wonder what happens to a rabbit when a cat inevitably catches one squeezing through the fence. Maybe the managers are fond of jugged hare for dinner, or maybe over-population is controlled by simply opening the gates of what I'd call their cage to the wilds of desert, where it all began.

10

Artful Encounters

"Beauty is altogether in the eye of the beholder."
Margaret Wolfe Hungerford, Irish novelist.

Before MS bombarded my body with its repeated attacks on my physical ability and my psyche, I pictured myself as a person who fit the adage 'Jack of all trades, master of none.' As a primary school teacher, a young and physically active parent, and an outdoor enthusiast, I figured I would find other interests to pursue when I got older and had more time. But the onset of my illness at age 42 directed me toward pursuing more sedentary interests sooner than planned. I decided that what I did with the rest of my life would be determined by my own decisions.

I was always drawn to art, thus I began taking classes in music appreciation, art history, literature (always a love), architecture, writing, and most recently, photo management on the computer—aptly fitting the "master of none" category! Those learning experiences, plus the role models and teachers I've known throughout my life have been a lasting help to me in overriding my disability.

The seeds for my wide-ranging interests were planted by my family in childhood, and if I may say so, are blossoming still. In addition to my parents, there have been others who've helped to foster and frame my life picture, from teachers to exemplary friends who have taught me the joys of learning, listening, and appreciating what is above and below the surface of a painting, a symphony, a building, or even a person's face.

As a high school freshman I'm not sure I knew what the word "empathy" meant, but I knew how it felt when I heard my classmates' nickname for my favorite English teacher, Esculene Anderson: 'Eagle-beak Anderson'.

"Eskie" was my parents' name for Miss Anderson, a bridge-playing college friend of Mother's who came to our home many times before she was my teacher. Recently I found her picture in my Robert A. Long High School annual. As a youngster I don't remember paying attention to her prominent Roman nose; it seemed to fit with her oval-shaped face and well-styled, grayish-white hair. She was stately, with kind eyes and red-red lips. She wore tailored suits and dresses with single strands of beads and matching earrings in ebony, jade, or pearl. As an adolescent I think I may have been more impressed by the way she was put together than by what she taught.

"Eskie's Seattle family is well off," Mother said. "In school we used to tease her about dressing up to go to class."

When I told my parents what the kids called her, Dad said, "Well, we've never served her corn-on-the-cob for fear she'd get her nose greasy." When Mother smiled I didn't know which one of them to be more upset with.

Miss Anderson made poetry fun, easy to read, and understandable. I loved listening to the rich, silvery tone of her voice when she read, "By the shore of Gitchie Gumee…" with its rhymes, rhythms, and alliterations. She tied that poem, Henry Wadsworth Longfellow's *The Song of Hiawatha*, to our study of the American Revolution in our history class, taught by Miss Jean Bell. For an A in English we could pick a section from Longfellow's poem and memorize a stanza. A few of these lines are still etched in my well-worn brain.

I suspect Miss Anderson was a closet smoker: her laugh had that deep throaty quality. But if she smoked it was well hidden by the perfumed scent of lilac on her clothes. When she read Emily Dickinson's nature poems, they spoke to me of my life. I also had a feeling for Tennyson's "Crossing the Bar," having heard it at Grandpa Keller's funeral.

When Wes and I lived in Bellevue during the fall of 1989, I learned that Esculene had retired to Seattle and was living in a condo by Lake Washington. I still had trouble calling her by her first name (she insisted) when I invited her to lunch, knowing she was housebound with macular degeneration. At a nearby restaurant she asked me to read the Daily Special, having memorized the rest of the menu.

"Are there errands you'd like to run?" I asked when we'd finished lunch.

"No. But if you'd like a short drive through the Laurelhurst District, I'll show you where I grew up and both my nephews' homes." Her driving directions were perfect, her memory faultless.

I told her she was my favorite high school teacher and thanked her for introducing me to so many fine poets and their works.

"I remember loving Emily Dickinson's nature poems," I said.

"I think I knew you'd liked them. Speaking of beauty, let's drive through the arboretum if you have time," Esculene said. "I can still see the changing colors when the sun is right."

I pulled the car over and slanted downhill, where the afternoon sun beamed through the maples and falling oak leaves. As if Esculene had the book before her, and in her wonderful metallic-deep voice she quoted,

> *"Nature rarer uses Yellow*
> *Than another Hue,*
> *Saves she all of that for Sunsets*
> *Prodigal of Blue,*
>
> *Spending Scarlet, like a Woman,*
> *Yellow she affords*

*Only scantly and selectly
Like a Lover's Words."*

I swear she could see my tears when she finished. "Thank you for an absolutely lovely day," she said.

When I was an undergrad at Oregon State, Gordon Gilkey's Visual Arts class was known as an easy A. There were few empty seats, since everyone had heard that the final consisted of simply naming painters and their paintings from a selection of slides he'd shown during the term, with every illustration included in the class text. Memorize the artists and their work and you couldn't miss the grade.

Before Professor Gilkey's class, my exposure to good paintings was nil except for three reproductions in our house: an eight-by-ten *Mona Lisa* over a chest in the upstairs hall, a large pastoral Constable above the living room sofa, and one of Vermeer's maidens pouring milk—which was, of course, in the dining room. Gilkey's class opened my eyes, stimulating my appetite for more of the huge world of art.

My first experience with famous paintings and other wonderful works came some twenty years later, in England, when Wes was an Air Force physician and we lived in the village of Stetchworth, a dozen miles from Cambridge's treasure trove. While we were house-hunting the first several weeks we were there, we lived on the Lakenheath Base. During that time my aunt and uncle from Montana took the train from London to Cambridge and accompanied us on our first visit to that city. Guide book in hand, we went first to Kings College Chapel, built in the 14th century, with the finest example of fan-vaulting in the world. The chapel's altarpiece, *The Adoration of the Magi* by Peter Paul Rubens, took our breath away. From that day on I was hooked. Cambridge became my favorite haunt, and every visit rendered a new discovery— a life-size sculpture of Lord Byron in the Christopher Wren-designed Trinity College Library, the sundial in the old court of Queens College, one of the few moondials in existence, medieval manuscripts at Trinity College, and an original Lord Byron poem, not to mention the stained-glass windows at Kings College Chapel.

After we were settled in our Stetchworth house, Edward and Emily Joy bought the Georgian cottage across the road from us. Edward had recently retired as curator of Ickworth House, a stately National Trust home in Suffolk. He'd had a long teaching career at the University of London and was the author of numerous books on furniture history. Before the Joys' arrival the villagers went on about the famous author soon to be in our midst. So after they'd moved in, I took over a bottle of California wine from the commissary and a bouquet of freesia. We were soon invited for drinks, and in their understated English way, they seemed genuinely pleased with my initial overture. Our relationship with the Joys blossomed into a long-lasting friendship.

The Joys introduced me to Cambridge's Fitzwilliam Museum. The collections covered Egyptian, Greek, and Roman antiquities, paintings, and drawings from all periods, plus many rooms devoted to the applied arts—ceramics, glass, and armor. Besides the fantastic collection of paintings by Rembrandt, Van Dyke, Gainsborough, Hogarth, and Picasso (to name a few), the museum has a richly ornamented cabinet by George Bullock, who Edward told us was the most influential furniture designer of the Regency Period (the first three decades of the 19th century). After a session where Edward had spent time showing us English 'buhl' (inlaid brass) and other period furniture decoration, including telling some of the Regency Period's history—that George IV was the Prince Regent until his mentally ill father, George III, died—Emily prodded him.

"Enough for today, dear," she said. "I need a gin."

"My wife keeps me from being a bore, I'm afraid," Edward said, as we walked toward the pub across Kings Parade for a late lunch.

I was never bored on any of the many day trips I took with the Joys around East Anglia: to Ickworth House where they'd lived as curators; to the Queen's estate at Sandringham, Norfolk; to London's Courtauld Institute Galleries, The Tate, The British Museum, and more.

Edward encouraged me to look upward to see the wonderful carvings and columns on the Fitzwilliam, designed by Basevi and decorated by E.M. Barry in the 19th C. If Edward taught me to look skyward, Emily focused on Cambridge's lovely ground-level gardens. She knew every

Cambridge College garden, their nooks and crannies, and importantly, the differing opening hours for each school.

With the Joys or with visiting company or even on my own, I spent as many hours as I could covering that amazing city.

After Edward's death in 1981, Emily moved from Stetchworth to Cambridge to be near family. On my first return trip to stay with her, we took flowers to Edward's grave. His tombstone read: "And gladly wolde he lerne, and gladly teche."

Once we were back in Eugene, I didn't take Father Allen Duston's Western Art Class at Lane Community College because of his good looks, but it helped. He resembled a handsome Greek athlete instead of fitting my stereotypical view of the paunchy priest. My guess is he wore his clerical collar in class to fend off any unattached women.

If Gordon Gilkey taught me what art was and Emily and Edward had shown me where to look for art, Father Allen, who at this time was also chaplain at Sacred Heart Hospital, showed me how to look at paintings, palaces, and architecture—particularly from the Baroque Period in Western Europe. Beyond his MFA thesis on the Dutch painter, Hieronymus Bosch (interesting choice for a priest—given Bosch's view that 'lust leads to internal damnation'), his interest seemed to lie with 17th century art.

Fr. Allen told us that the early Roman Catholic Church expected paintings and sculptures in its edifices to speak to the common person. With his slide presentations he showed how 17th century artists explored and created their paintings from repeated patterns, lots of details, and the use of bright colors.

"The main goal of Baroque art was to give the viewer a sense of awe," he said.

And that it did. Every time I visited Kings College Chapel and saw the Reubens *Adoration of the Magi*, I felt the same wonder and awe as when Wes and I were at the Prado in Madrid. I'd written a paper for Father Allen's class on Diego Velazquez, and when we walked into one particularly magnificent room in the museum, I encountered my favorite Velazquez painting, *Las Meninas*. There it was in all its glory, life-sized, richly textured, and all-encompassing on the huge wall: in the foreground, the child-princess, Margaret, the court-jester dwarf, a dog, the painter, working at his easel on images of the king and queen as seen through the reflection in a mirror. I felt a personal connection with that painting from my studies and somehow also felt that I knew what life was like in Phillip IV's court with his painter, Velazquez, who died at age sixty-one.

So it is with continued amazement and respect for the fullness in my life that I give thanks to my teachers—to those who are now gone and to those who continue to help me in my continued pursuit to be a "Jack of all trades."

II

My Dream House

Longview, my hometown, lay about an hour's drive from Spirit Lake, Washington, up a majestic two-lane road along the Toutle River that was hemmed on either side by thick and stately Douglas fir. As far back as I can remember, my family spent a week each August vacationing at Spirit Lake. The first few years we camped out. Afterwards we rented a cabin across the lake from the then-intact Mt. St. Helens at Harmony Falls Resort. I went to camp at Spirit Lake as a youngster, then became a counselor and, following that, the camp hike master. At seventeen I had my first real job at Harmony Falls Resort. I'm still in love with that long-gone place and cherish the memories of it.

I knew I couldn't marry someone who didn't share my love for this part of the world, so when Wes and I became engaged, I conned my parents into inviting him along on their annual Spirit Lake vacation, though all three balked. My parents had hoped to have the days alone with me. Wes was reluctant to take even a weekend away from his summer job with a Portland construction company. The money he made in the summer with that company plus working several jobs during the school year in Corvallis paid for his entire four years at OSU. I persisted, determined to know that he shared and cared about my feelings for this place.

I got my way. Wes followed me into that glacial lake with a coltish leap of faith, and the wedding was on. Today Wes backs off from anything wet that's below eighty degrees Fahrenheit, and that's fine with me. But that day at Spirit Lake, he said something like, "It's a bit chilly but otherwise okay." I took his understatement for approval. From then on I dreamed of living next to a lake and, 35 years later, I got that wish.

When Wes and I were looking for a place to call home in Oregon after living in Bellevue for two years, we rented temporarily in Eugene rather than make a hasty decision. I was elected to house hunt as Wes was working full time. So, with my most prudent and practical friend Katherine in tow and almost free rein to look, I headed for the coast and Florence, Oregon.

I walked into what was then the Coast Real Estate office cold turkey and asked to see lake-front property. I'm not sure how Katherine and I ended up with agent Jim

Hoberg, a recent licensee and not much older than my son, Tom. Perhaps he was assigned to us because I didn't look like a serious prospect with my dirty gray van and its cooler full of cheese, crackers, apple slices, trail mix, and sodas. No time to waste eating out! Actually, the cooler made a hit with Nike-clad Jim. He favored the Peanut Butter Cups that Katherine said we shouldn't be eating because of our MS. See what I mean about her prudence? Anyway, Jim laughed and said it reminded him of family car trips he'd been on as a kid and the kind of food his mom would come up with when one of his siblings asked, "Are we there yet?"

"I want to see lakefront property at either Woahink or Mercer Lake. Nothing up on a cliff or with a batch of steps," I told Jim.

"There's not much on Woahink that doesn't involve stairs or a trail. Maybe a couple of possibilities. We'll go there first since we're close, but I'm sure you'll find Mercer more accessible," Jim said, glancing at the cane tucked under the seat behind me.

Turns out that Jim was partial to Mercer Lake because he grew up there. His parents still lived there, and he hoped to buy there when he sold enough property to people like me.

As we turned off Highway 101 toward Woahink Lake and drove down the narrow, unpaved road through a large grove of fir with a sprinkling of rural mailboxes and the smell of wet cedar in the air, I thought, *This is it*. We pulled up in front of a cottage-style smoke-gray house with white trim and an evergreen clematis climbing across the garage toward an upstairs window. A huge hemlock cascaded over the circular drive, and a native dogwood that was at least a hundred years old stood in the center, surrounded by raised beds trimmed in white azaleas and millions of blooming bluebells. The café curtains were open, and I could see that the lake front lay across the entire back of the property—completely "au naturel."

When Wes first saw the lake and the property filled with huckleberries, fuchsias, pines, and cedars, he could have bet that I didn't even look inside the house. My mind was clearly made up. But he wasn't so easily seduced.

Neither Jim nor Katherine would let it go at that. With characteristic patience and practicality, Katherine pointed out the glitches: Originally a two-bedroom cabin, the house was the oldest one on Ford Way; the additions probably weren't up to code; Jim couldn't tell us the age of the septic tank—and so on. Jim cautiously suggested I might be happier with something new and up-to-date, and that the woodstove in the kitchen was really just for looks.

We proceeded to look at several new houses on the Siuslaw River. Jim pointed out that everything north of town (Woahink being south) had city water and utilities. Katherine thought we should take a look at a brand new house on Collard Lake, but we both decided it was too citified. Her feelings were colored by her Collard Lake family history: In the fifties and sixties, Katherine and her husband, Bruce, camped there with their four children. She reminisced about her kids rolling down the sandy dunes into the lake by the hour, building fires to roast hot dogs and marshmallows, and eating huckleberries until their lips were stained purple. We agreed that the citified changes wouldn't work for her or me!

Her father-in-law used to own the lake and its surrounding property, which he sold for $65,000 in the mid-sixties to take his wife on a European trip. In 1991, the Collard Lake house Jim showed us was priced at $200,000 and the neighbors were within spitting distance.

It took me the better part of two months and a batch of arm-twisting to convince Wes that he would have fun repairing what I called minor problems in his free time and taking care of a few major ones that kept turning up during the five years before we remodeled.

In some ways, having that cottage by the lake those twelve years seems like a dream. A major plus was being able to forget my MS disability or at least put it on the back burner much of the time we were there. I didn't have to walk far to get where I wanted to go.

My electric scooter took me up and down the road, around the wooded lanes, and on to the many accessible parks and trails in the area to hunt mushrooms in the fall and look for nesting waterfowl in the spring. I swam daily in the lake for four or five months and exercised in the pool house the rest of the year. I kayaked on the lake whenever the weather permitted.

I felt healthy and whole there—planting a raised vegetable garden in the southern side-yard, picking salad ingredients in the early morning's cool, and re-living some of my girlhood alongside my granddaughters, Esther and Micki. They would tell you that the best summers of their lives were spent at 5111 Ford Way. And, except for my memories of Spirit Lake, Washington, me, too!

Patty, Esther and Micki about 1994

12

Kayaking, Friendship, and Fate

It's best to kayak on Woahink Lake on a summer morning, since the afternoon winds are often lusty and changeable. The morning sun's rays had just touched the water and a hush hovered over the tiny riffles that Ingrid's skiff and near-silent motor made as she crossed the lake. As she approached our dock, the sun's rays made a yellow-golden tail that wagged off the stern of her boat. I took it as a happy sign and grabbed her lead rope to tie it to the mooring cleat.

"Greetings! It looks like we're in for another good outing," I said, thinking both of the weather and the fast friendship we had developed over several decades and many hours together—sharing our life stories while skimming the lake.

My kayak is a safe, ocean-going, two-person rig that sits low and steady in the water. Its light Kevlar construction (like the fiber used in bullet proof vests) makes it very strong but easy to navigate. I sat in the rear that morning, with my feet on the pedals that attach to the rudder. When I pressed down the kayak turned like a dancer.

"Ocean going" implies salt water, but the only sea water my easy-riding Beluga (its trade name belies its shape and blue-and-beige exterior) had touched was the Siuslaw and Siltcoos estuaries. When the kayak was new, Wes and I took a class at Sheldon pool to learn how to right her if we tipped over. Standing on one side of the kayak, we bounced in the water for dear life. She finally tipped to our combined 300-plus pounds, but not easily.

Even though the kayak is as stable as a waterbed in a sandbox, I'd long since given in to Wes' insistence that I wear a life vest. So, with our life preservers secured and the kayak steadied, Ingrid and I decided to cross the center, widest part of the lake, heading east toward the Summerbelle arm, then south and shoreward to an unoccupied area—no homes, docks, or people in sight. Once we reached the opposite side, we lazed close-in, exploring the shoreline that ranged from deep and fir-lined to shallow and sandy, careful to avoid the wind-toppled snags fingering the shore. It wasn't unusual on such a morning to hear the slap of a beaver's tail ducking into the water or the shrill sass of a stellar jay as we passed by her thicket.

The morning sun was fully up as we inched into a relatively shallow area that was imbedded with water-slogged logs and chalk-colored snags scattered about like huge pick-up sticks. Precious little light reached that wet wood, which as a consequence produced the grassy mosses and lichens that are usually saved for swampy forested areas.

Ingrid noticed some pea-green knobs protruding from the log grass. *Chameleons? Geckos?* We inched in for a closer look. Voila`! They were bog-dwelling cobra lilies, technically named Darlingtonia Californica, and more commonly called California pitcher plants.

I probed lightly, sticking a blade of grass between the hairs inside the plant's head. It snapped like a trap around the blade. I felt a tweak of what Darwin may have experienced, discovering a new species.

"In my 40-plus years of exploring around this lake, I've never seen a single cobra plant," Ingrid said with delight.

"Aren't we fortunate to have shared this together?" I said, imagining that women who'd grown up with sisters would know and understand my feelings.

It might have been that day on the lake that Ingrid told me an incredible story. During WWII, when the Germans were occupying the war-soured country of Norway, she was working as a nineteen-year-old stenographer for the Bergen Steamship Company.

As Ingrid typed in her enclosed glass cubicle, a

terrible crash occurred and the building crumbled all around her. A freighter full of munitions had been docked in Bergen's nearby inner harbor, and the explosives were ignited, perhaps by a welding spark. She was temporarily blinded and was sure the Germans had bombed the building and vicinity. Despite the death and destruction that engulfed the entire area—including life-threatening injuries to the woman in the cubicle next to hers—Ingrid was miraculously spared. The blast was so powerful that buildings crumbled and ships were washed ashore.

I can only guess at how living through such a tragic and frightening experience, and coming away physically unharmed must have affected the rest of her life. Ingrid is amazingly compassionate woman. I've seen her live each day with exactness and wonder. I would imagine we both marvel at how much fate has influenced our lives.

On another of those days kayaking together, I talked openly with Ingrid about the most difficult and on-going heartache for Wes and me: our son, David, had been diagnosed with schizophrenia when he was 20, old enough to be able to accept or reject the psychiatric help that we so desperately tried to provide for him. We had lost our fun-loving, academic, and athletic middle son to a hideous disease that robbed him of the full and good life that I felt sure was his destiny.

David spent more years than I can bear thinking about as a homeless person, riding the rails, and hitch-hiking across the country and back, returning home only when he became desperate, hungry, and too sick to manage on his own. He was finally hospitalized, and has recovered. He's now able to manage his medical needs and have his own apartment in Eugene. He is a good cook who helps me shop for local produce, runs errands for me at Costco, and helps both of us with yard chores. The state-paid jobs David does for several clients at the Laurel Grove Apartments, where he lives, gives him a sense of security and brings me peace of mind.

Years earlier our family had stopped at the Darlingtonia Botanical Wayside north of Florence to walk through the boggy, shaded area protecting clusters of California pitcher plants—the same species that Ingrid and I had encountered that morning on the lake. After seeing

Patty and Ingrid, 1998

David's fascination with the strange plants, I decided to buy him a similarly carnivorous Venus Flytrap for his eleventh birthday. For ages he tended that plant in a terrarium in his room, feeding it live spiders and other (probably dead) insects he found outside. He still retains the same keen interest in science that he had as a kid and recently told me that Venus Fly Traps are now an endangered species.

What part of personal good fortune—when accidents happen or diseases such as David's and mine strike and when the ups and downs of life occur—can be attributed to fate? If friendships are formed somewhat by chance and enriched both by choice and by accident—such as living close to a lake, like Ingrid's and mine—I often think about what other roles destiny has played, not only in my life, but in those of the people I know and love.

13

Down Ford Way

Bill, the man who bought our house on Ford Way in Florence, Oregon, invited us to dinner while we were staying at his cousin's house nearby. The two properties are less than a fourth of a mile apart. The terrain between them is a flat, narrow, graveled lane—perfect for getting around on my scooter.

When we'd purchased the property in 1991, spring was in full bloom. White azaleas edged the circle in front of the cottage, and bluebells carpeted the ground in an area between a wild quince, red huckleberry bushes, and native Rhododendrons. For me it was love at first sight, an infatuation that lingers on.

The hand-carved cedar *Private Drive* sign that our son Doug gave me the first Christmas we spent there was still nailed to an old-growth fir on the right of the driveway, far enough from the four end-of-the road mailboxes so there would be no mistaking which lane it indicated. When Doug had replaced its "Private Property" cardboard predecessor, he said, "Tacky isn't you, Mom."

I glanced down the heavily wooded road, loving the way the firs seemed to hover and protect the huckleberries lining the needle-padded lane leading to the circular drive. There had been a light rain earlier in the day and the scent of wet moss, fir boughs, and hemlock made the air feel fresh and clean. I'd hoped Bill would be busy inside so my husband, Wes, and I could poke along, taking a good look, secretly knowing that nothing nature or we had done to the place during our years there could possibly be improved on.

Where the drive forks we had pruned a huge rhododendron back to make room for an oversized hot-tub house in the center of the circle. In the six years we'd been away, the shrub had leafed out to its original lushness. The calla lilies I'd often divided and given away had multiplied and shot up like Roman candles along the sides of the pool structure. Their white-funneled blossoms and thick shiny leaves complimented the pink blooming rhododendron, almost hiding the pool house from the road.

An earlier occupant had planted a honeysuckle and an old-fashioned red rose climber. The two vines wove like lovers up the lattice next to the garage. I knew I had no business asking Bill what happened to the honeysuckle, whose blossoms smelled like a touch of heaven every spring, or mentioning how the rose looked scraggy and unhappy without its former partner, but that's the honest truth.

To the right of the front patio, the evergreen clematis still rambled along the side of the house and across the

View from my kitchen window, about 1993

top of the garage roof, a permanent fixture that, with a good pruning twice a year, knows and keeps its place. The Tropicana climbing rose that Wes planted to be seen from both sides of the bedroom window was full of buds and healthy foliage. Bill obviously liked roses.

As a would-be landscaper, my taste runs toward the English-cottage look (Wes calls it messy). Once I saw a fall-blooming clematis on Whidbey Island climbing profusely across a barn door, intertwined with a lovely yellow rose. I bought a start of the plant and stuck it in next to the Tropicana. The following August the new clematis had spread along the front rain gutter. I loved the way its leaves rippled in the wind like sandpipers fluttering along the ocean shoreline. During August and September, the vine produced clusters of white-star flowers that dangled above the window. When I was seated at my desk with the window open, the flowers smelled of sweet carnations.

The replica of a lion-faced, bronze statuary doorknocker that I brought from Durham Cathedral in England (it was said that anyone who grasped the knocker was under the church's protection) and nailed onto the front door had been backed with sponge padding to muffle the sound. When we rang the doorbell, Bill's golden retriever had a barking snit. Before I toed the threshold her message rang clear—*This place is mine now!*

Bill had spent his working years overseas with the East Asia Corporation. His collection of artworks and artifacts from that part of the world fit nicely in the house. Not much could change the inside coziness of two brick fireplaces, wood mantles, and knotty pine walls. The windows in the bedroom, family room, and kitchen all face the lake. When the house was ours, my eyes were always oriented toward the water. The day of our visit was no different.

Inside, the first thing I noticed from my family-room seat was the missing hemlock that had filtered the morning sun though the un-curtained bedroom window. I used to love waking up in summer as the sun rose behind the trees lining Woahink Lake.

Bill sounded apologetic: "Since the hemlock was so close to the foundation (it had been about 6 feet from the bedroom window), I was afraid its growth might damage the house. I'm sure you folks thought of that when you remodeled." Bill said, "Now I'm afraid I made a mistake."

"The builder said it could damage the roots when we moved out the foundation. We even had an agreement clause relieving him of responsibility for that tree," Wes said.

"The cedars had to go—they were diseased—but I'm sorry about the hemlock," Bill said.

I sat there feeling like a tree-hugging, bird-loving member of the Sierra Club, remembering all the flocks and species that had entertained us from that spot. I doubted there would be many feathered friends to watch now, with Bill's two house cats hanging around and fewer places for the birds to nest or perch.

One spring dawn years before, an amorous rufous-sided towhee had persistently beat his beak against the bedroom window pane, sure that his reflection was a would-be mate. He would hop around in the salal and huckleberry bushes below the hemlock and then fly up to the window, back and forth. After several days of his early-hour tenacity, I put two butterfly stencils on the inside of the pane. That was one determined bird. He merely moved a window to the south and began pecking at the family room glass. I decided to face the inevitable, bought some ear plugs, and gave up.

Another visitor, with more considerate midday hours, was a northern flicker who fed with the same noisy persistence on the Port Orford cedars close to the lake bank. The cedars were dying up and down the coast of a root disease, making them easy prey for woodpeckers and interesting for us window-watchers.

That bird's favorite cedar looked like a black bear might have stripped the bark at its base. Higher up, the flicker's dogged drilling in the peeling bark left holes, like she had been using it for target practice rather than food-getting. I don't blame Bill for having the cedars removed nor for the fact that he couldn't possibly know what he was missing.

Outdoors, I had felt comfortable, but inside there was precious little left for me but memories, especially of the times spent there with our granddaughters, Esther and Micki, who summered with us when they were six and eight until their high school years. The girls would come home from Girl Scout Camp at Cleawox Lake to Ford Way, singing the same camp songs I'd learned at Spirit Lake, Washington, when I was their age. Esther, Micki, and I loved to swim and kayak together on the lake. The girls went belly-wopping (riding on inner tubes) behind our speedboat, fished off the dock, and pan-fried their catch with Grandpa Wes.

Change is inevitable. Over the years I've observed that the happiest people are those who can adapt to that unalterable fact. I'm doing my best to be among them. Our granddaughters are young women now, making their ascent into adulthood. They seem to accept life's changes as naturally as the seasons.

If they should ever walk down Ford Way to this place we all loved, they will have memories similar to mine. Perhaps one of them will even put pen to paper to try to capture their past, just as I am trying to do.

A Leave Taking

The memories are sweet my friends
says the magnet on my fridge
stuck there through openings and closings
eleven chock-full years
the foodstuff of notions and spills
glued like pearls into my life's shell.

I want to remember
the tangy spring smell
of wet hemlock and fiddlehead fern
and the gold and house finches feeding
teetering, challenging one another.

I want to remember the summer's sunrise
glinting through Ponderosa and Douglas Fir
where dwarf bunnies hid
behind the woodshed
and under celery-green salal.

I won't forget how osprey cheeped all summer
from sun-up to dusk, loud and brassy
or the electric surprise as my fingers
touched August's still-cold water.
Headfirst and thirsty I drank it all in.

14

Kipu Ranch Adventure

When I phoned to ask for a guided tour of the three-thousand acre Kipu Ranch on Kauai, I inquired whether walking was involved. After trial, error, and more than thirty years of living with MS, I'd learned that more doors opened when my mouth stayed shut.

The woman who answered said, "No walking. We'll put you on a Mule."

"You mean like riding a horse?" I said, ready to forget it. She laughed. "You'll be on an ATV—All Terrain Vehicle."

Mule sounded slow enough. Maybe that would be better than the ATV Bomber or Rhino pictured on the brochure.

"I've got you down for 1:30," the receptionist said.

You never know what you can do until you try, and it can't be any worse than riding a snowmobile or dune buggy. Wes opted out. "My back wouldn't tolerate the first five minutes on one of those contraptions," he said. "I'll take pictures of you in your dirt shirt when you get back."

The ad read, "See the film locations of 'The Lost World' and 'Raiders of the Lost Ark,' in a stable, friendly, fully automatic Honda 400 ATV." I wasn't hooked on the transportation mode, sci-fi dinosaurs, or Indiana Jones, but both films had been shot on the Kipu Cattle Ranch in the Hule'ia Valley. This ranch is the third-largest privately owned property on the island and had previously been inaccessible to tourists. If riding with a guide on an ATV tour was the only way to get there, well, this physically challenged woman was ready.

It was the second sunny day on Kauai since we'd arrived. It occurred to me as we crossed a one-way bridge over the muddy Hule'ia River and wound down an unpaved road through more than one big splash that I might be underdressed in my white tee, Capris, straw hat, and sandals. When we pulled into the parking lot and I took one look at the dozen or so mud-caked ATVs, I wondered if this time I'd bitten off more than I could chew.

With a few misgivings, I signed my name and the date three times to a two-page disclaimer stating that Kipu Ranch Adventures was not responsible for accidents. *Broken bones, crushed legs and arms, death?* I was given a bandana to cover my face and then followed the other six paying riders to a shed to be fitted with helmets and goggles, wishing I'd brought my parka along.

Our two guides were Milt, a pale, skinny Caucasian kid with a thick blond pigtail resting between his narrow shoulder blades, and Sammy, a well-built native with the entire Hawaiian Island chain tattooed down the middle of his rippling brown back. The two guys alternated roles as head guide. Sammy led off after going through the rules of the ride.

"Number one: Keep your legs and arms inside your rig at all times! Number two: Never grab the gas lever to hang on. That's what these grab bars are for." There were more rules, but since I was the only passenger in a vehicle with double seats in front, I figured they didn't apply. Besides, it was a struggle to hear what Sammy was saying because my helmet and chin-strap fit like an undersized girdle.

"You're the unfortunate babysitter?" I said to my driver, Milt, exacting a shrug. "Where should I put my cane?"

"Behind the seat," he said, eyes dead-set on catching up to the other five ATVs that had already moved out. He closed one of the six cattle-guard gates we would pass through during the next three hours and got up to 21 mph as we raced down a dry, rocky lane lined with dozens of tall, winter-green Norfolk pines (any faulty descriptions are due to speed and my determination to act laid back).

"How're we doin?" Milt asked, coming to a stop where the others were already off their ATVs awaiting us.

"Perfect," I said, loosening my grip on the grab bars, unbuckling my seatbelt, and stepping outside the rig to look at an incredible, sweeping view of the valley below. There was a heavy cloud cover over Mt. Wal'ale'ale, one of the rainiest places in the entire world according to the guide books. *Wow! This is why I'm here!*

"Is this ATV a mule in disguise?" I said, looking at the camouflage-painted hood and mud-caked fenders.

"Souped-up army rig. You name it," Milt said, nodding toward Sammy who was telling area history to the other six customers.

"In the early 20th Century Hawaiian royalty sold 1400 acres of this property for $3000 to the Rice family. The rest was deeded by the owner, John T. Waterhouse, to his family at his death, to be divided among his four nieces and one nephew. One part lives on this side of the mountains. The other side of the family owns that over there," he said, pointing toward the ocean and another range of jagged volcanic peaks.

"We'll go there later. This is a working cattle ranch. Once they raised sugar cane. Back then there were 150 employees living here during the harvest."

"Questions? Okay, we're off," Sammy said.

'We're off' meant following the others one by one, hell-bent through scrub brush, pastures of grazing cattle, and on to another scenic stop, where we dismounted and everyone except me removed their helmets. I tried, but my chin strap wouldn't budge. I turned my helmet sideways. All that did was loosen my earring. It dropped in the grass and was retrieved by a well-seasoned biker-type guy who was probably thinking, *this old lady doesn't have a clue.*

Meanwhile, Milt was at the trail edge, holding a delicate, daisy-like blue flower from a small bush and giving a flat, samey description without audience eye contact. With my hampered hearing, I picked up that the plant came to the islands with the Chinese, who used it as a cure-all.

The ATV in front nearly tipped over!

Dried in tea or mixed with alcohol, it had the effects of Valium and Laudanum.

Alongside the possessed daisy was a small, airy fern. When touched it retracted—a carnivorous bug catcher. And there was more. Milt muttered names that sounded like "Kapu, Hilo-Hilo, Hueja" or the like. Don't quote me. I'd be the last to tell him to look up and speak up if he wanted to be considered learned.

Then we were off again, with what seemed like a competition between drivers as to who could make the loudest ROOM, ROOM! We went lickety-split over ruts and ridges and then followed a well-notched passage surrounded by thick foliage and trees whose trunks were grounded by low branches and roots that looked like the bars of an imaginary jungle-prison. With my eyes closed it felt like riding a carnival roller coaster.

I almost swallowed my tongue when we screeched to

a halt a mere two feet from the edge of a high ledge that dropped off into wet red dirt about 14 feet across, with ruts as big as the man-sized moguls I'd once snow-plowed through at Lake Tahoe—sure that I'd never make it to the bottom. From our perch we watched Sammy demonstrate for his group how to descend that mountain of rutted mud that curved out of sight into the seemingly never-ending jungle.

Besides me the group consisted of three couples. Two were on double ATVs, riding motorcycle style, the woman behind the man. The other was a more proficient pair riding on single rigs. After Sammy finished discussing the disastrous effects of falling off and finding oneself crushed between the machine and the mud, he asked for a volunteer.

The littlest woman on the single, who couldn't have weighed more that 100 pounds soaking wet, raised her hand, "Here!"

With her on his rig, Sammy gave a painstaking demonstration of exactly what and what-not to do. That feisty woman rode it out, like the ATV was her dancing partner and Sammy a tango instructor.

I sat there watching the other three drivers going through the same torture before taking off, feeling thankful that I wasn't at the wheel of our *Mule*. In the past, what my husband referred to as my cavalier approach to being disabled had worked. I tried not to worry about things I had no control over. I hoped this upcoming mudslide wouldn't be my final gumption test.

After the last ATV had safely gone on, Milt said, "Ready?"

"Go for it," I said. We got down the cliff without me falling out or throwing up. I felt hopeful that this would be the final test of my will—that is, until I spotted the group dismounted at the top of a wide trail on the other side of a streamed full of milk-chocolate water. I could feel it coming. Milt hit the gas and in we went. Muddy water shot out, up, and sideways like a mixed-up hailstorm.

"Eeeeeek," I said, as he gunned the accelerator again and again. Then Rrrrr—ump.

"Stuck," he shouted, turning off the motor and high-tailing it straight through the stream toward the rest of the group, with water splashing inside his calf-high boots.

Alone, I took a deep breath, closed my eyes, and let my body go limp. The feeling of acquiescence that I'd worked on being able to access at will since my MS diagnosis years earlier kicked in. I sat still with my seatbelt tightened, thinking—challenged or no—being at someone else's mercy isn't always that bad. Mid-afternoon, 79 degrees, plenty of strong arms. The worse scenario (for them) would be carrying me across the creek to dry land and retrieving the ATV later.

When would I ever have an experience like this again?

An attempt at shoveling watery mud below the tires didn't work. Next Milt attached a winch secured by ropes to my newly-named Bronco Buster and onto a single rig in back. The guy who found my earring took the driver's seat next to me. As he gunned it, we bucked up and down, with Sammy ramming the front bumper, Milt pulling from the back, and me hanging onto the grab bars as if my life depended on it. This was better than riding a horse or mule, except for the dirty water slopping over the floorboards! The others were about 25 yards away. As our four-wheeler freed and we surged forward to the other side and dry land, the group cheered like we'd just won Olympic Gold.

I tried hard not to show my relief! I'd signed on knowing I was in for some excitement, but I had had enough for one day. Unfortunately, our money's worth meant three more stops. I sensed I wasn't the only one who could have done without Sammy's rendition of Harrison Ford high in a Kukui tree, rope-swinging over the Hule'ia River.

From the river we backtracked and drove southeast across a lea and what seemed by then pretty tame ground. As we climbed uphill toward the volcanic range of jagged peaks that surrounded a coastal inlet, I began to get my second wind. At the mountain's pass we stopped by a gated dirt road that dropped slowly, cascading toward a pasture and onto two coves with secluded white-sand beaches.

In this age of Hawaiian high-rises, the scene below was make-believe. No wonder Hollywood chose this lovely ranchland for movies.

"There's a great photo op from up here. Unfortunately, it's no trespassing beyond," Milt said, scrambling up a short path to the right of the gate after I'd handed him my camera.

"Who lives there?" I asked. Not a building in sight.

"Caretakers. They're cool," he said—whatever that meant.

We wound downhill at a slower pace past cactus-like plants and white poppies outcropped from lava rock.

I'd hoped for a little more botany or bird identification, but that didn't happen. Down a well-traveled lane with an expansive valley view and clouded mountains in the distance we went, catching up with the group, already off their ATVs, their cameras flashing.

Then the grand finale: a large herd of wild, hairy pigs with long bushy tails and mud-caked, suction-cup-snouts the size of baby bottles. There was a pushy black boar, suckling babes, and at least three sows in shades from black/brown to white with a dozen tame peacocks mingling in. The pigs clustered close to Sammy's feed bag, snorting and searching the mud puddles as he scattered seed about, helter-skelter. These weren't the aggressive beasts I'd heard about. They were just plain piggy!

Wes was waiting to snap my picture when we arrived back in the parking lot. I was definitely wearing a dirty shirt, but, what the heck, there was nothing a warm bath and plenty of soap couldn't cure. At the end of the day, I was happier than a pig in mud. Exhausted, yes, but no bumps or bruises to cloud my memory of an unforgettable Kipu adventure.

Mud spots never came out of the clothes!

15

Wake Up Call

Change sometimes hits like a sneaker wave, knocking you over with a shock—the death of a loved one or friend, a car accident, a son's divorce. Aside from those times in my life, I've often moved into a new phase before being aware of leaving a former one.

In the spring of 2008, I ended up in the hospital for two weeks with pneumonia, causing my first relapse in many years. The changes that followed me home from the hospital are now routine. The sole step in our one-level house now sports a grab-bar, and the shower has three. My handy rod with pick-up tongs and a magnet on the end works great for retrieving the stuff I'm constantly dropping—tissues, paper clips, peanuts, and even hearing aid batteries.

I'll admit that vanity kept me from having a walker (or thinking I'd ever need one), but my rehab therapists wouldn't let me leave the unit without the blessed thing. It's become my in-house assistant that packs around grocery bags, newspapers, books and laundry. It even has locking arms so I can convert it to a chair if necessary. I don't trip and fall as often as I did when I had only a cane to aid me. *'I'm learning to make do with what I have left.'*

The happiest people I know are those that can adapt to change, since change is unavoidable and there are no alternatives. I was a slow learner during the first years of my illness. Accepting the inevitable was difficult, to say the least. One of the hardest parts of living with my disability was giving up the athletic pursuits that had been a major part of my identity.

Being disabled has some similarities to growing old. Those who leave the doors open to previous friendships and social life while developing new pursuits and relationships get along better than others who are glued to the TV and the status quo. In the beginning I wanted family and friends to treat me as before—to let me take charge of myself and make my own decisions. I was determined not to be a physical cripple, nor did I want anyone (including Wes) to feel they had to be there when I tripped up. I wanted to tough it out on my own.

The problem that kept coming up (and still does on occasion) was that what I felt was realistic for my circumstance didn't always seem right or reasonable to others. When my mother overstepped the boundaries I'd drawn, I could understand, but having well-meaning friends make decisions on my behalf without consulting drove me up the wall.

"Won't that be too much for her?" my worried mother asked Wes when one of my seminar goals was to look for a travel agency job.

The part-time work I found at Valentine's Travel consisted of more hours than I had anticipated, plus transporting and transferring the quadriplegic owner, Dan, and his wheelchair on job-related errands in my car. It became an exhausting challenge, but at least I gave it a try and succeeded enough in my own mind to bow out after a year, tired, but more realistic about my capabilities.

My curtailed social life depressed me somewhat until I learned to make concessions for the people I cared about outside my family. I finally adapted to a new persona (one that didn't need constant company for reassurance) and found that I not only enjoyed the freedom of being alone, but that my disability could be an asset.

On a perfect retreat at Cascade Head, where the Salmon River Estuary flows into the Pacific, I partnered with the instructor in her two-person kayak. Sammie was a dynamo redhead with the chutzpah of an Olympian. I didn't sense that the other ten participants were put out by my disability when they'd give me a hand getting in and out of the kayak. The second day we put into the Nestucca River near Pacific City, paddled downstream to the ocean, and ate lunch on a sandbar, waiting for the tide to switch.

"Want to try my single on the way upriver?" one of the men said. "Give me a go with the boss-lady."

"Sure," I said, taking it as a compliment that the strongest man in our group thought I was capable of paddling a single upriver.

A few years later I went alone to a writing workshop in Santa Fe, bringing along a lightweight scooter that came apart for transporting. By chance, there was only one cab waiting at the small airport. With luck, the driver was a burly young man with a van large enough to transport my scooter and bags. Besides assembling the wheelchair, he drove me to the conference and insisted on seeing me inside before he took off. After five days of workshop and tooling around Santa Fe in my electric wheelchair, Wes met me with a rental car, and we headed north for Rancho Jacona. The Rancho was accessible, private, and had a pool plus beautiful gardens. I'd taken a chance on the flight into Santa Fe's small airport, on the workshop being productive, and on the Rancho (found in a guide book) being a good vacation spot. We'd go back to in a minute.

I realize now that it's hard for those who aren't around me all the time to take my needs into account, but I'm still perplexed and annoyed by many reactions I get from seasoned friends. Some think it's their right to decide when my illness allows me to participate or be included in outings. I might not be able to hike five miles with a group, but I'm game to show up at the end with a packed lunch and drinks. I've finally learned to make my needs known to others and to be more assertive, avoiding unnecessary "shoulds." I try to stay away from relationships that I've moved beyond or outgrown.

Even so, it's taken years for me not to feel paranoid about being left out. I don't know how many times I've said I'd rather be a spectator watching a friend play tennis than sit at home feeling lonesome and sorry for myself.

Today one of my biggest dissatisfactions is that I can't walk unaided for any distance farther than half a block. I guess I could say that's a step forward after over thirty years of living with MS. Aging has given me an outlook advantage: that of having a more suitable attitude toward my disability and a vent for my frustrations.

I don't believe it was luck that was responsible for the good in my lifetime—or the bad stuff, either. "Into every life a little rain must fall." My rain came on in my forties like a waterfall. Bad luck or simply the luck of the draw?

As I look back, I continue to move forward, knocking on wood that the waterfall remains a trickle and that lightning won't strike wherever I choose to park. Life is good today. Age and disability continue to open the doors for more goal-setting. I'm still feeling *good to go*—well, most of the time.

Paula, an occupational therapist at Sacred Heart Hospital's Rehab Unit, came home with me to offer suggestions for my in-house and garden safety needs after I was hospitalized for two weeks in 2008. I had had pneumonia and a frightening MS relapse, my first in ages. She suggested installing grab bars in the shower, handles beside the step from the garage into the house, and clearing out all the scatter rugs, including my favorite, a rectangular prayer-sized rug with an oak leaf and full-flower design. The rug's muted shades of burgundy and green blend perfectly with our kitchen's dark mahogany cupboards, plus it catches the drips from the dishwasher and kitchen sink.

"I'm just here to make suggestions," Paula said when she saw my grimace. "I can see you'll do as you please."

Entering the swimming pool for the first time after I'd come home, I thought about what Paula had said. "Go in backwards holding onto the bars as you step down." I backed in until the water was waist high, laid back with my arms spread-eagle, and folded into the warm water until it buoyed under me, ruffling over my body. This is how I like to stay for a minute or so, feeling light and relaxed.

For the next few weeks after my relapse, my morning water-exercise routine was limited to half the time I usually spent in the pool. After my initial float that first morning, I dropped my legs, rolled onto my tummy and took several strokes to the pool's north edge. Standing sideways, I grabbed my outside ankle and pulled back and up as hard as possible. Rather than counting my stretch minutes, I looked with affection at the five Tuscan lavender bushes lining the pool's north edge. They were bursting with fresh new sage-green bristles. I felt free and happy to be home and healing.

Five years earlier, the "lavender lady" from Hamm

Road, southwest of Eugene, had delivered five Number Ten pots of graceful French lavender. Before we planted them, Wes and I mulched, added lime to the soil, watered, and then placed the bushes in a row with space between for the foliage to mound and spread. By June their fragrance had replaced the spicy smell from the daphne bush that each year has helped me get through the January/March cold-edge that hovers outside the pool.

But this morning was warm. I grabbed below my bent knee, pulled up and out to the side, and held it taut while counting the tree swallows swooping high in the sky. Their numbers had doubled in the two weeks I had been away. As usual, the local scrub jay was hanging around, checking me out from the neighbor's newly opening cherry tree. Slowly I swam to the steps in the deep end to flutter and frog kick, hanging onto the bars. The anjou pear that Wes had espaliered onto the side of the pool shed several years ago was in full blossom, and the lilac in the northeast corner was ready to burst with perfumed flowers.

I grabbed my synthetic barbells, one in each hand, crossed my legs at the ankles, and rolled onto my back, looking at the patches of blue sky surrounded by cloud fluff. The neighbor's birch was waving thousands of fingerling catkins below the rising sun. *You're home, and spring, like you, is slower this year, but it's coming.* I pushed to the left with my arms taut and made circles, twisting my lower body from the waist down, counting to 20—then repeated in the other direction. The barbells serve as buoys. Usually I'd bicycle with them tucked at my sides under the water and/or do my version of pumping iron (knees up, then push forward with my arms extended as my legs go back), but for now I was taking it easy on myself, remembering my doctor's advice.

My legs were telling me to go slow, so I tucked the barbells under the step handles and called it enough for one day. Since the sidestroke is effortless, I ended with a few laps, admiring how well the arborvitae hedge surrounding the entire back yard had fared after its fall trimming.

Morning in the water is my time alone to plan my day, to think through a writing project, to prioritize—something I'd been told many a time I needed to work on. In the hospital, Dr. Rugani, my pulmonologist, suggested something good might happen as a result of my bout with pneumonia and the scare I received from the MS relapse.

"Your energy and strength will return to your norm, but it will take time. Don't push yourself," he said.

But, given my Northwest background and my parents' recreational orientation, it would be impossible to change my life's outdoor focus. In the heat of summer, when it's too hot even for swimming, this heavy-hedged enclosure makes me long for the open woods or for a trail alongside a river or lake. My need to feel unfenced gets very thirsty.

On that warm, windless morning, seven goldfinches (five flashy golden males) flew from the feeder by the pool when I showed up. They perched and watched me from the crabapple, their plumage combining with the magenta blossoms to make a spectacular blaze of color. What I have here in my own backyard is lovely, though different from our Woahink Lake woodland cottage where red and blue huckleberries, firs, and salal lined the drive and the only urban noises came from the motorboats on the lake.

The tamer, suburban pleasures I'm finding in my Eugene backyard are things like bees busying in a pair of flowering blueberry bushes, two fig trees with limbs of budding fruit, or a rufous hummingbird having breakfast outside the kitchen window. It is with renewed respect that I continue to watch the seasonal changes surrounding me daily.

In my mid-seventies, as my strength grows slowly back to normal, I ponder how I can make my future as full and rewarding as it has been in the past.

No price tag can be attached to the love, caring, and support I've received throughout my life from family and friends, and the spring of 2008 was no exception. My illness has helped me appreciate what's at my fingertips. With a heart full of gratitude, I'm anticipating the future with promise.

Why are so many of us surprised when the inevitability of change occurs in our lives? I've long since recovered from pneumonia and the MS setback. The wake-up call I received from that scare reminds me once again that changes are unalterable. What we do with what we have in the present makes for happiness.

I'll do my best to continue to adapt, and to look for the good in this ever-changing life of mine.

David, Tom, Doug, Wes and Patty, Christmas at Ford Way, 1996

www.ingramcontent.com/pod-product-compliance
Lightning Source LLC
Chambersburg PA
CBHW022304060426
42446CB00007BA/479